NEW TYPO-GRAPHICS

++++ WITH ++++ FONT SAMPLES

PIE BOOKS

NEW TYPOGRAPHICS WITH FONT SAMPLES

PIE BOOKS
2-32-4, Minami-Otsuka, Toshima-ku, Tokyo 170-0005 Japan
Tel: +81-3-5395-4811 Fax: +81-3-5395-4812
e-mail: editor@piebooks.com sales@piebooks.com
http://www.piebooks.com/

ISBN4-89444-393-7 C3070
Printed in Japan

NEW TYPO-GRAPHICS WITH ++++++++++ FONT SAMPLES

Contents

Introduction

Today, the rise of Macintosh and the spread of graphic software make it relatively easy to create new fonts.
The world of typography changes from day to day as various kinds of fonts are produced.
The traditional familiar fonts such as Helvetica and Futura, the digital fonts developed recently by Emigre or T-26,
and the fonts designed to look like handwriting...
You can find a number of typefaces and typography everywhere that have so many different approaches and forms:
some of them have an impact on readability, while others focus on creating a unique look as a character.
On the other hand, there are many more graphic works that adopt handwriting instead of regular fonts,
and thus it generates the diversity of recent typography.

This book aims to present the current state of typography, showcasing a lot of high quality typographic works
with strong visual appeal around the world, especially graphic designs using new digital fonts.
Works introduced are grouped in four categories:

■ Commercial Font: which can be purchased.
■ Custom Font: designed for companies, usually not for sale.
　　　　　　　Also the fonts converted from existing typefaces are included in this category.
■ Free Font: distributed free of charge.
■ Others: handwriting fonts and characters made by hand.

The credit data includes the designer name, type of work,
and country originated as well as the category mentioned as above and the font name.
It also contains the URL address where to purchase or download these fonts, and besides,
the font sample (alphabets from A to Z and numbers) is introduced as far as possible.
The section, from pages 129 to 160, features only font samples so that you can see them in larger size.
(Page numbers indicated in the credit data correspond to pages showing samples.)
Approximately 80 samples are introduced by category in this section.
(Please note that some fonts are presented only in sample pages.)

We hope that this volume will serve as a valuable reference source of typography
and typefaces and inspire the creation of logomarks and typesetting.

We would like to send our most sincere thanks for designers who contributed work
to this book in spite of their busy schedules.

はじめに

Macが台頭し、コンピュータソフトが普及した現在、以前よりも比較的容易にフォント制作ができるようになりました。

様々なテイストの書体が現われ、タイポグラフィの世界は日々変化しています。

ヘルベチカやフーツラなど古くからある伝統的な書体や、エミグレやT-26など近年開発されてきたデジタリックな書体、

あえて手書き風に制作された書体……可読性や実用性を重視したもの、

それよりも文字としてのユニークさを重視したものなど、実に様々なアプローチの、

様々なかたちを持ったタイプフェイス、及びタイポグラフィを、いたるところで見つける事ができます。

一方、最近ではフォントを用いずに手書き文字を使用したグラフィック作品も多く、現在のタイポグラフィの多様性に拍車をかけています。

本書はそうした「今の時代のタイポグラフィ」をテーマにした作品集です。

デジタリックなフォントを用いたグラフィック作品をメインに、世界中からクオリティが高く、

ビジュアルアピールの強いタイポグラフィを多数収録しました。

作品のカテゴリは使用フォントの種類により、以下の4つに分類しています。

■市販フォント(Commercial Font)：購入可能なフォント。

■非売フォント(Custom Font)：企業のためなどに制作されたオリジナルフォントで、通常は非売のもの また、既存のフォントをアレンジしたものも含む

■フリーフォント(Free Font)：フリーで配布されているフォント。

■その他(Others)：手書き文字や、ハンドメイドによる文字など。

作品クレジットとして、制作者名・アイテム名・国名などのほかに、上記カテゴリと書体名を記載しています。

また購入先・ダウンロード先のURLを併載すると共に、フォントの書体見本(A-Zまでのアルファベット及び数字など)も可能な限り掲載しました。

巻末129〜160ページにはフォントサンプルだけのページを設け、大きなサイズでフォントを見ることができます。

クレジット部分にリンク先として参照ページ数を記していますので、ご利用ください。

フォントサンプルページには、フォントのみ紹介のものも含め、カテゴリ別に計約80書体を掲載しています。

タイポグラフィ及びタイプフェイスの資料集であると共に、ロゴマーク制作や文字組などのアイデアソースとしても活用いただけれは幸いです。

多忙な中、快く作品をご提供いただいたクリエイターの方々に、深くお礼を申し上げます。

LOOK FORWARD, NEVER BACK

A view on modern typography ——————— VIER5

We are increasingly aware of a growing interest in the contemporary use of lettering and modern typography.
This becomes especially clear in places where one wouldn't normally expect cultural innovations:
in urban space, on the street. To be more precise, we are talking about graffiti.
Not the graffiti which we are familiar with since 1970, but its further development.
Highly complex word and language systems, carried out with tape, glue and poster paper, or simply with chalk,
can be seen along city streets, leaving behind their content-related but also graphical messages.
Quick and uncomplicated works. Design, reject and alter, a simple method that produces jumps in development at breakneck speed,
creates new habits of looking and reading, and is able to expand and change our understanding of typography.

A large part of this new generation of graffiti stems from artists, and many of the students we teach at various universities
are intensively dealing with this form of communication. Initially conceived more as a form of communication,
it now proves to be highly interesting for the development of new typographical elements,
because it creates signs that tread new typographical paths and can point to the future through both content-related and technical phenomena.

Unfortunately, many institutions, like leading museums, magazines or fashion houses,
don't seem to take notice of this important phase of origin of new typographical messages.
In the worst case, they are completely oblivious of it. Here, people still shrink from dealing
with contemporary typography (probably because of a certain fear of the unknown).
One prefers to rely on (deceptive and questionable) values that appear secure. Regretfully,
these institutions are increasingly situating themselves outside of a contemporary context worthy of discussion,
since the application of customary forms of typography seems to be less and less suitable to harmonise with modern architectural developments.
For example, it does not seem to keep pace with or to do justice to highly complex artistic and sociological structures.
With regard to the typographical developments of the 1990s, one notices with horror that it takes 6 to 10 years before innovative developments
in the field of typographical design become generally accepted and used.

Apart from these regrettable structures, one must reasonably say: We no longer build like we did 30 years ago,
we don't dress in the same fashion as 30 years ago, so why should we still write like we did 30 years ago?
This is the starting-point of a new generation of typography, guided by the idea of shaping the future creatively and meaningfully.
The objective is to create a new form of typography that aims at replacing outdated standards,
which turn out to be more and more anachronistic and useless, with new signs that are valid and respond to contemporary structures.

To this end, a pioneering spirit and pioneering work are, of course, required.
But with a growing understanding of art and fashion, as well as of cultural and social issues,
the view on the use and application of typography has also changed.
It is no longer only seen in the context of decorating image material with information, and now its justification no longer lies solely in its legibility.

Nowadays, typography is increasingly seen as what it really is: an independent and autonomous art form. And like any other form of free artistic expression,
modern typography has all existing possibilities at its disposal to express itself.
This takes place in a range starting with what is normally regarded as applied, all the way to dealing with experimental or abstract typography.

At the same time, working with typography is also scientific research work, research in cultural as well as sociological areas.
Developing typographical structures is close to exploring contemporary social and cultural trends and influences.

But the aim should always be to create an independent typographical identity that is strong enough to describe the phenomena
and forces of the respective period in a clear and precise way.

This publication is meant to promote the joy of typography and to motivate people to deal with typography in a free and undaunted way.

Paris;; Nov/Dec 2004

Profile: VIER5

A design-studio, founded 2002 in Paris by Achim Reichert and Marco Fiedler.

The work of VIER5 is based on a classical notion of design. Design as the possibility of drafting and creating new, forward-looking images in the field of visual communication.
A further focus of our work lies on designing and applying new, up-to-date fonts.

The work of VIER5 aims to prevent any visual empty phrases and to replace them with individual, creative statements, which were developed especially for the used medium, partner or client.

http://www.vier5.de

前を見つめ、決して振り返らない

現代のタイポグラフィに関する見解 ——— VIER5 (フィーア・フュンフ)

以前にもまして私たちが注目しているのは、レタリングや最新のタイポグラフィを現代風に使用することに対して関心が高まりつつあることだ。

特にこれがはっきりと現われているのは、普通は文化的な新しさが期待できない場所、つまり都会の空間の路上である。

もっと明確にいうなら、グラフィティのことを指す。それも1970年頃からよく見慣れている落書きのことではなく、さらに進化したやつだ。

テープや糊、ポスターの紙を使ったり、またはシンプルにチョークで書かれた、かなり複雑な単語や言語のシステムを街の道路沿いに見ることができ、

書かれた内容に関連したグラフィカルなメッセージを残している。素早く作られた簡単な作品だ。

デザインとは、拒絶され改造され、猛烈なスピードで急速に進化していくシンプルな手法であり、

見ることや読むことの新たな習慣を創り出し、そして私たちのタイポグラフィに対する理解を押し広げ、変化させていく。

この新しい世代のグラフィティのほとんどはアーティストが始めたものであり、様々な大学にいる私たちの教え子の多くが、こうしたコミュニケーションの表現に深く関わっている。

初めはコミュニケーションのひとつの形態以上のものと考えられていたが、今では進化した新しいタイポグラフィの要素としてかなり興味深いものとなっている。

なぜなら、非常に優れた内容や技術を通して、新しいタイポグラフィの道を切り開き、未来を暗示することができるサインを作り出しているからだ。

あいにく、先端を行く美術館や雑誌、ファッションブランドといった多くの機関は、新しいタイポグラフィのメッセージの発端となるこの重要な面にあまり注目していないようだ。

最悪の場合、まったく気付いていないことすらある。現代のタイポグラフィに関わるのを嫌がっているのだ (おそらく、知らないものに対する畏怖の念からだろう)。

人は、信頼できそうな (見かけ倒しで不確かな) 価値感を当てにしたいと思うものだ。

残念なことに、こうした機関は、自らを議論すべき現代のコンテクストの外側に位置付けたがるが、

その理由は、この日常的なタイポグラフィの形態の用途が、現代の建築の発展とは調和しない傾向にあるからだろう。

例えば、それは複雑で芸術性の高い社会構造と共に歩んでいるようにも、その中で正しいことをしているようにも見えないのだ。

90年代のタイポグラフィの発達を振り返ると、タイポデザインの分野における革新的な進化が一般に受け入れられ、

使用されるようになるには6年から10年かかるということに気付き慄然となる。

こうした嘆かわしい状況とは別に、当然こう言う人もいるだろう。

「30年前と同じような建築はしないし、30年前と同じファッションをまとうこともない。なら、どうしていまだに30年前と同じように字を書かなくちゃならないんだ?」

これこそが、未来を築くアイデアによって創造的かつ有意義に導かれた、新世代タイポグラフィのスタート地点だ。

時代遅れで使いものにならなくなった古い基準を、現代の構造に対応する正当で新しいサインに置き換えるための、タイポグラフィの新しい形をつくり出すことが目的だ。

これを達成するには、確かにパイオニア精神や先駆けとなる作品が必要だ。

しかし、文化や社会問題に対する理解だけでなく、アートとファッションに対する理解が深まるにつれ、タイポグラフィの使用や応用に関する考え方も変化してきた。

それは、もはやイメージ素材を情報で装飾するというコンテクストの中だけにとどまらず、現在ではその正当性さえも可読性の中だけに存在するものではない。

最近では、タイポグラフィの真の姿がますます理解されつつある。タイポグラフィは、他に依存しない独立したアートなのだ。

そして、芸術的で自由な他の表現と同じように、現代のタイポグラフィには自由に表現するためのすべての可能性が備わっている。

本来実用的と思われることから生まれたものが、実験的または抽象的なタイポグラフィというすべての方向へと広がっていくのだ。

同時に、タイポグラフィをあつかうことは、社会学や文化の分野におけるリサーチなど、学問的な探究を行うことでもある。

タイポグラフィの構造を開発することは、現代の社会や文化の流行やその影響をじっくりと調査することだ。

しかし常に目指すことは、その時代の現象や影響力をはっきりと説明できる十分な強さをもった、独立したタイポグラフィのアイデンティティを創りだすことであるべきだ。

本書は、こうしたタイポグラフィの楽しさを伝えるとともに、自由で大胆なやり方でタイポグラフィに取り組むための原動力となるだろう。

プロフィール: VIER5 (フィーア・フュンフ)

アキーム・ライヒャートとマルコ・フィードラーによって2002年にパリで設立されたデザイン・スタジオ。

VIER5の作品は、デザインの古典的な発想を元にしている。デザインとは、ビジュアル・コミュニケーションの分野における、新しく未来を見据えたイメージを描き、創り出す可能性だ。
また彼らの作品がさらに重視しているのは、最新のフォントをデザインし、取り入れることにある。

VIER5のデザインが目指しているものは、ビジュアルの空虚な表現を避け、またそうした表現を、パートナーやクライアント、すでに使われている手法などに合わせて特別に展開した、
個性的でクリエイティブなメッセージへと置き換えることだ。

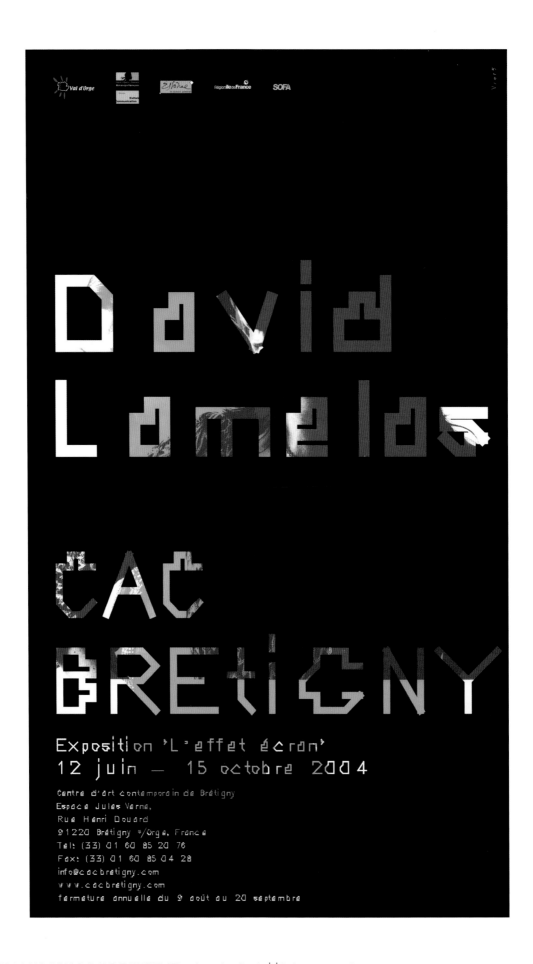

ABCDEFGHIJKLMNOPQRSTUVWXYZ abcdefghijklmnopqrstuvwxyz

Commercial Font   F 062aPlotter-Achtundzwanzig   http://www.forhomeorofficeuse.com

Poster 2004 France   CL: centre d'art contemporain de bretigney (CAC bretigny)   D, DF, SB: VIER5

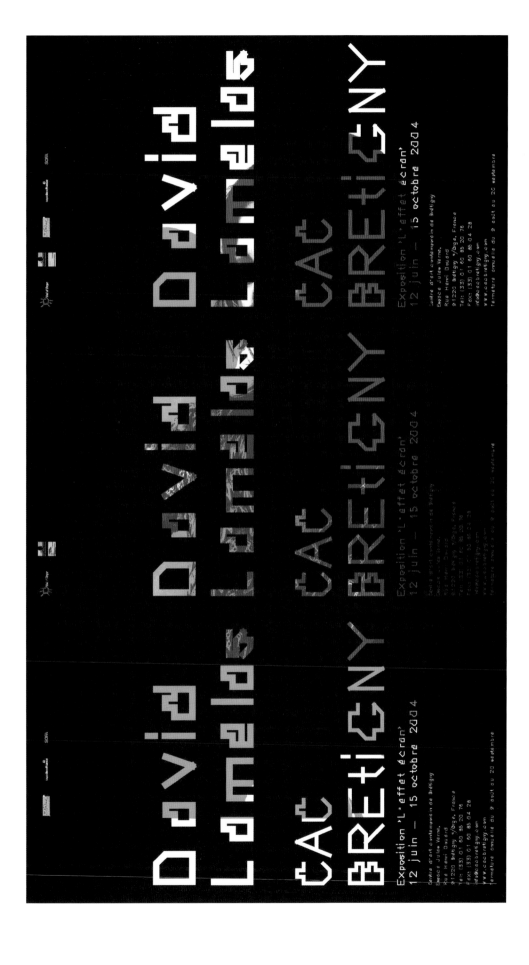

ABCDEFGHIJKL MNOPQ RSTUVWXYZ abcdefghijklmnopqrstuvwxyz   ♀ p130

ABCDEFGHIJKLMNOPQRSTUVWXYZ abcdefghijklmnop   ♀ p133

Commercial Font   ⊞ 062aPlotter-Achtundzwanzig / 062aPlotter-Bandzug / 1Try   ⬇ http://www.forhomeorofficeuse.com

Poster 2004 France   CL: centre d'art contemporain de bretigny (CAC bretigny)   D, DF, SB: VIER5

Pavillon du Palais de Tokyo et
s-Walter Müller

tar, Pascal Beausse, Louidgi Beltrame, Davide Bertocchi,
Bock, Olivier Dominici, Sophie Dubosc, Johannes Fricke-
ausen, Shiho Fukuhara, Agnieszka Kurant, Ange Leccia, Christian
st, Hans-Walter Müller, Gaël Peltier, Gerald Petit, Jean-Luc
h, Music performances: Armand etc

Centre d'art contemporain de Brétigny
h-18h Espace Jules Verne, Rue Henri Douard y
17h Tel: (33) 01/60 85 20 76 91220 Brétigny/Orge France
www.cacbretigny.com

Pavillon du Palais de Tokyo et
s-Walter Müller

tar, Pascal Beausse, Louidgi Beltrame, Davide Bertocchi,
Bock, Olivier Dominici, Sophie Dubosc, Johannes Fricke-
ausen, Shiho Fukuhara, Agnieszka Kurant, Ange Leccia, Christian
t, Hans-Walter Müller, Gaël Peltier, Gerald Petit, Jean-Luc
h, Music performances: Armand etc

Centre d'art contemporain de Brétigny
h-18h Espace Jules Verne, Rue Henri Douardy
7h Tel: (33) 01/60 85 20 76 91220 Brétigny/Orge France
www.cacbretigny.com

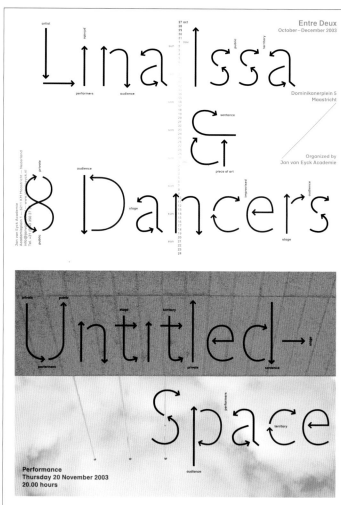

Custom Font **F** Helm

Poster 2003 Netherlands   CL: Jan van Eyck Academie   AD, D, DF, SB: Sulki & Min Choi

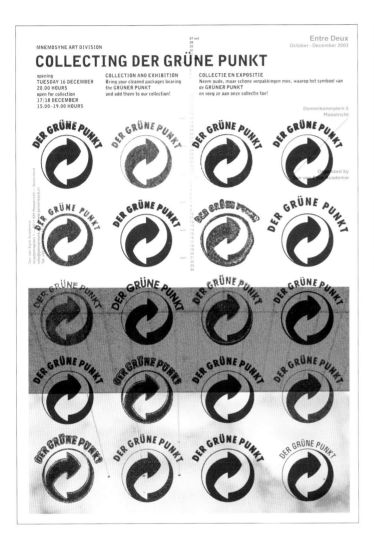

02/09/01

ANOTHER
DAY
IN
THE
MONTH

Q: WHAT HAPPEND ON 2 SEPTEMBER 2001?

A: NOBODY REALLY CARES.

02/09/01 PAGE A+B

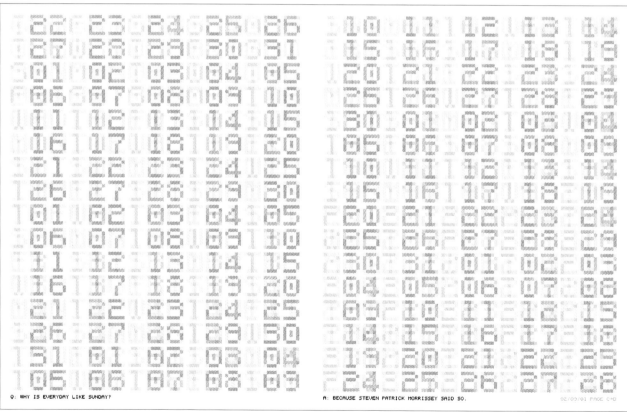

Q: WHY IS EVERYDAY LIKE SUNDAY?

A: BECAUSE STEVEN PATRICK MORRISSEY SAID SO.

02/09/01 PAGE C+D

Custom Font   ▪ Custom made for this project

Book 2001 Netherlands   CL: Class Work   AD, D: Min Choi   DF, SB: Sulki & Min Choi

THIS DATE HAS MOVED TO PAGE F-6

SLEEPSLEEP
SLEEPSLEEP
SLEEPSLEEP
EAT   WORK
WORK   WORK
WORK   EAT
WORK   WORK
WORK   WORK
WORK   EAT
WORK   WORK
WORK   WORK
SLEEPSLEEP

Q: 9-2=7 AND 9+2=11, HENCE '7-ELEVEN'. WHAT DO YOU THINK IT MEANS?

A: NOTHING BUT YOU ARE A PARANOID.

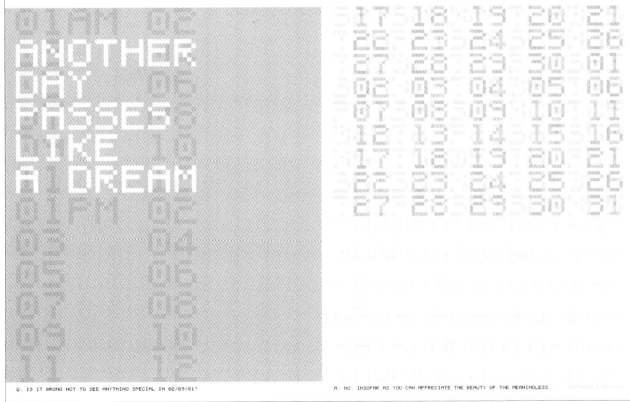

ANOTHER
DAY
PASSES
LIKE
A DREAM

Q: IS IT WRONG NOT TO SEE ANYTHING SPECIAL IN 02/09/01?

A: NO, INSOFAR AS YOU CAN APPRECIATE THE BEAUTY OF THE MEANINGLESS.

ABCDEFGHIJKLMNOPQRSTUVWXYZ abcdefghijklmnopqrstuvwxyz

Free Font — Tartan font / Kabel — http://www.tm-online.nl

Poster 2003 Netherlands CL: TM AD, D, SB: Richard Niessen

Free Font   File Sharing font / Kabel   http://www.howtoplays.nl

Poster 2003 Netherlands   CL: TM   AD, D, SB: Richard Niessen

p157

Artis Ad de Jong en Jonas Ohlsson ABCD Slogan Mixed Interest Font Poster

Free Font   Constellation font / Kabel   http://www.tm-online.nl

Poster 2003 Netherlands CL: TM AD, D, SB: Richard Niessen

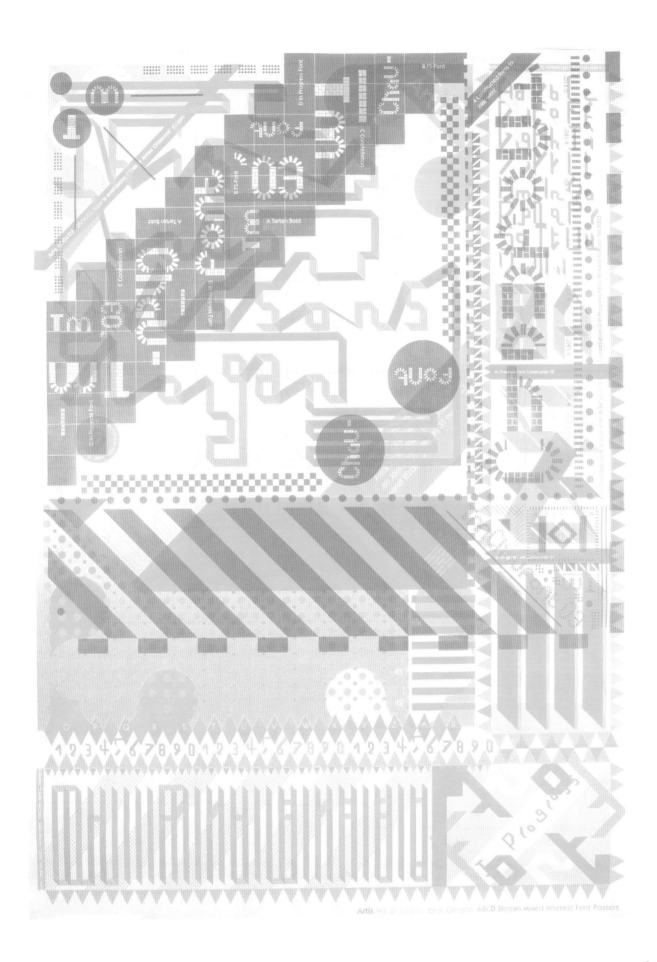

Artis Poster Lot of fonts ABCD Slogan Mixed Interest Font Posters

ABCDEFGHIJKLMNOPQRSTUVWXYZ abcdefghijklmnopqrstuvwxyz

Free Font   In Progress font / Kabel   http://www.tm-online.nl

Poster 2003 Netherlands   CL: TM   AD, D, SB: Richard Niessen

Poster

Custom Font | ARBM font / Horatio

Poster, Brochure 2002-2004 Netherlands CL: ARBM, Art at Governmental Property AD, D, SB: Richard Niessen D (Poster): Harmen Liemburg

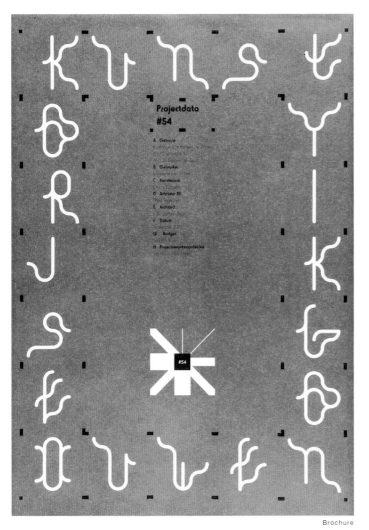

Brochure

Brochure

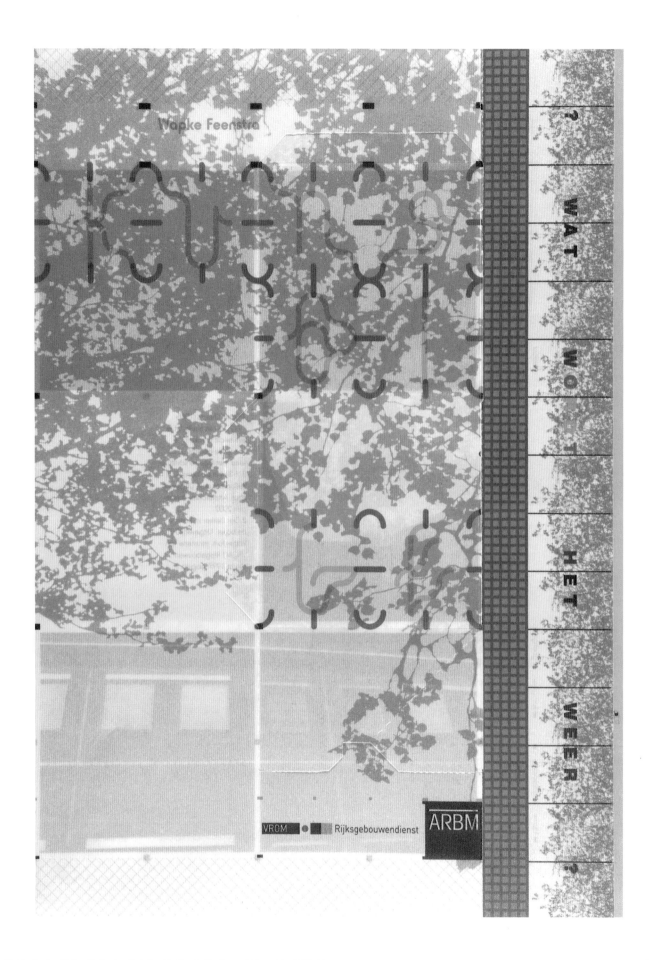

Wapke Feenstra

WAT WORDT HET WEER?

VROM · ■ ■ Rijksgebouwendienst

ARBM

Custom Font ▪ ARBM font / Horatio

Brochure 2003-2004 Netherlands CL: ARBM, Art at Governmental Property AD, D, SB: Richard Niessen D (p024): Yolanda Huntelaar

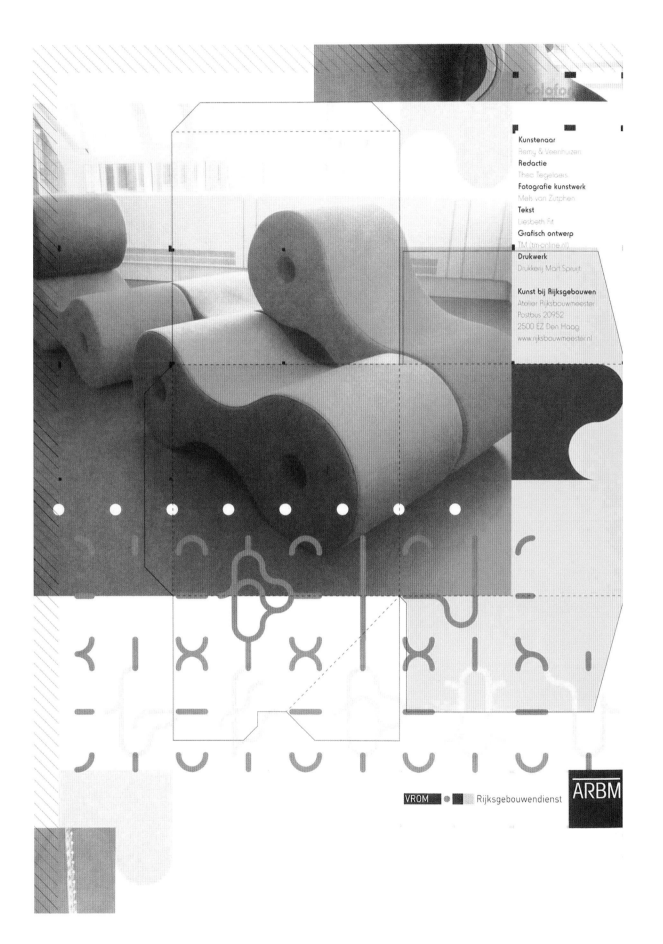

Kunstenaar
Remy & Veenhuizen
Redactie
Theo Tegelaers
Fotografie kunstwerk
Mels van Zutphen
Tekst
Liesbeth Fit
Grafisch ontwerp
TM (tm-online.nl)
Drukwerk
Drukkerij Mart Spruijt

Kunst bij Rijksgebouwen
Atelier Rijksbouwmeester
Postbus 20952
2500 EZ Den Haag
www.rijksbouwmeester.nl

VROM Rijksgebouwendienst

ARBM

Commercial Font F Champion

Poster 2004 France CL: Humanite AD, DF, SB: Studio Apeloig D: Philippe Apeloig

Commercial Font   **F** Franklin Grotesk Condensed / Gravur Condensed

Poster 2004 France   CL: AFAA, Association Française d'action artistique   AD, DF, SB: Studio Apeloig   D: Philippe Apeloig

UN
TRANS CHOIX FORUM
PORT STRATÉ ÉCONO
FLUVIAL GIQUE MIQUE

Commercial Font   Foundry Sans

Poster 2003 France   CL: Voies navigables de France   AD, DF, SB: Studio Apeloig   D: Philippe Apeloig

13-20 MARS 2004
9E SEMAINE DE LA LANGUE FRANÇAISE
ET DE LA FRANCOPHONIE

/amertume///
//bouline///
///brousse/
déambuler//
/espérance/
farfadet///
//lumière//
ombellifère
/tactile///
/tataouiner/

Commercial Font   Gravur

Poster 2004 France CL: Ministère de la culture et de la communication AD, D: Philippe Apeloig DF, SB: Studio Apeloig

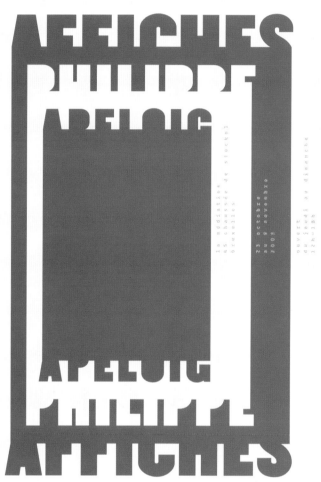

Commercial Font ☐ Champion / TAZ

Poster 2004 France   CL: Fête du livre, Aix en provence   AD, DF, SB: Studio Apeloig   D: Philippe Apeloig

Commercial Font ☐ Champion / Fago monospace

Poster 2003 France   CL, AD, DF, SB: Studio Apeloig   D: Philippe Apeloig

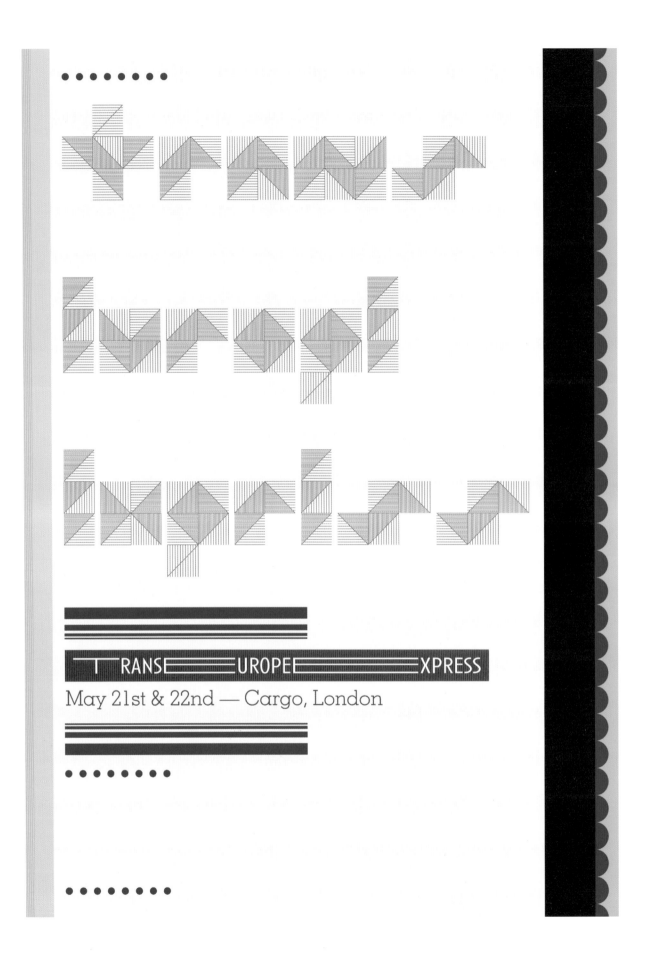

TRANS EUROPEE XPRESS

May 21st & 22nd — Cargo, London

Custom Font   Custom made for this project / Memphis

Flyer 2004 Finland   CL: Trans Europe Express Festival   AD, D, I: Teemu Suviala   AD,D: Antti Hinkula   DF, SB: Syrup Helsinki

Custom Font   F Custom made for this project

Page Illustration 2004 Finland   CL: Image Publishing / Muoto magazine   D, I: Teemu Suviala   DF, SB: Syrup Helsinki

Custom Font | Beauty Font

Poster 2001 Japan   AD, D, SB: Takeshi Hamada   I: John Peters

504destruct

brett calzada
lectures at Columbia college

april 27 2004 7pm
623 S Wabash Ave 4th Floor
Chicago IL 60605

ABCDEFGHIJKLMNOPQRSTUVWXYZ abcdefghijklmnopqrstuvwxyz

Commercial Font   F Millionaire   ⬇ http://www.final.nu
Poster 2004 U.S.A.   D, P: Brett Calzada   DF, SB: 504destruct

Poster 2004 U.S.A. CL: School of Visual Arts AD: Silas Rhodes D: Stefan Sagmeister / Irina Thaler / Paul Rustand Retouching: Steve West DF, SB: Sagmeister Inc.

A B C D E F G H I J K L M N O P R S T U V W X Y Z a b c d e f g h i j k l m n o p

ABCDEFGHIJKLMNOPQRSTUVWXYZ

Commercial Font 1Try / FT-Bold http://www.forhomeorofficeuse.com

Magazine Cover 2004 France D, DF, SB: VIER5

A B C D E F G H I J K L M N O P Q R S T U U W X Y Z

Commercial Font | F Lini-DreiEo | http://www.forhomeorofficeuse.com
Poster 1999 France D, DF, SB: VIER5

Custom Font   Ⓕ Custom made for this project
Poster, Postcard 2002 Japan   CL: TAKEO   AD: Naoki Sato   DF, SB: ASYL DESIGN

Custom Font   Ⓕ Custom made for this project
Poster 2003 Japan   CL: PARCO MUSEUM   AD: Naoki Sato   DF, SB: ASYL DESIGN

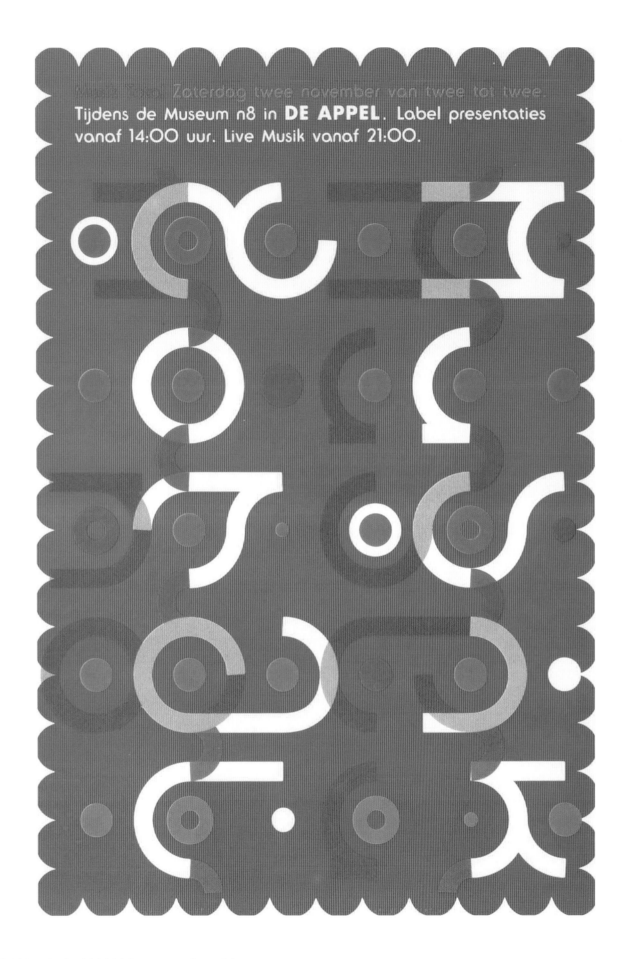

Free Font   File Sharing font / Ronda   http://www.howtoplays.nl
Flyer 2002 Netherlands CL: The Appel AD, D, SB: Richard Niessen

ABCDEFGHIJKLMNOPQRSTUVWXYZ abcdefghijklmnopqrstuvwxyz

Free Font | In Progress font / Futura | http:www.tm-online.nl

Poster 2003 Netherlands CL: TM / Vasava, Barcelona AD, D, SB: Richard Niessen

Custom Font | Alphabet for the Amsterdom Old Church

Poster 1999-2001 Netherlands CL: Stichting De Oude Kerk Amsterdam D, DF, SB: Atelier René Knip

STICHTING DE OUDE KERK TE AMSTERDAM

HET INTERNATIONAAL STEENWINKEL ORGEL FESTIVAL 2001

25 AUG. GUSTAV LEONHARDT

1 SEPT. MATTEO IMBRUNO

8 SEPT. LORENZO GHIELMI

15 SEPT. YUZURU HIRANAKA

22 SEPT. JAAP ZWART

29 SEPT. HARALD VOGEL

DE OUDE KERK

AANVANG 20.15 UUR • Entree f15,-Euro 6,80. CJP/stadspas/65+ F10,- Euro 4,54. Studenten gratis

Kaartverkoop tevens bij de AUB Ticketshop en via De Uitlijn (0900-0191) f 0,88 cpm. / 0,40 Euro pm.

STICHTING DE OUDE KERK TE AMSTERDAM. 1012 GX AMSTERDAM. TEL 020.6258284 • FAX 020 6200371. okadam@xs4all.nl • www.oudekerk.nl

Mogelijk gemaakt door Steenwinkel Kruithof Associates Amsterdam

---

STICHTING DE OUDE KERK TE AMSTERDAM

ORGEL À L'IMPROVISTE!

2 MAART GIJSBERT KOK
ONDERMEER BUXTEHUDE EN MENDELSSOHN

9 MAART JAN HAGE
ONDERMEER REGER EN ALAIN

16 MAART HAJO BOEREMA
ONDERMEER HINDEMITH EN MESSIAEN

23 MAART TOON HAGEN
ONDERMEER KEE EN WELMERS

AANVANG 15.00 UUR • ENTREE € 7.- • CJP/PAS 65/STADSPAS/STUDENTEN €4.60

DE OUDE KERK

De Oude Kerk te Amsterdam / Oudekerksplein 23 / 1012 GX Amsterdam 020 625 82 84 / www.oudekerk.nl / E-mail: info@oudekerk.nl

Kaartverkoop tevens bij de AUB Ticketshop en via De Uitlijn (0900-0191) 0,40 € pm.

Mogelijk gemaakt door Amsterdams Fonds voor de Kunst en Steenwinkel Kruithof Associates Amsterdam

Ontwerp Atelier René Knip

WERELDPREMIERE

TANGO WALTZ

♛♛♛ DON 20 + VRIJ 21 JAN 05

CONCERTGEBOUWORKEST

WAGENAAR

ROBERT SPANO, DIRIGENT
ALEXANDER KERR, VIOOL
WERKEN VAN D.WAGENAAR
SALONEN EN BERNSTEIN ING 🦁 🎵 N‖ON PHILIPS

KAARTVERKOOP 020 671 83 45 » WWW.CONCERTGEBOUWORKEST.NL

SKRJABIN

LE POÈME
DE L'EXTASE

♛♛♛ DON 30 SEPT + VRIJ 1 OKT 04

CONCERTGEBOUWORKEST

OLIVER KNUSSEN, DIRIGENT
LEILA JOSEFOWICZ, VIOOL
WERKEN VAN LINDBERG
KNUSSEN EN SKRJABIN

 ING 🦁 🎵 N‖ON PHILIPS

KAARTVERKOOP 020 671 83 45 » WWW.CONCERTGEBOUWORKEST.NL

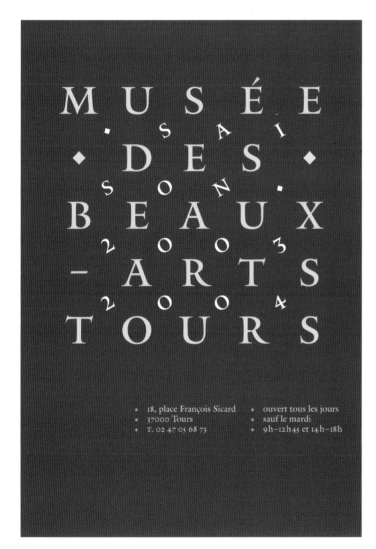

Commercial Font ⓕ Galliard

Poster 2003 France   CL: the Museum of Beaux-Arts of Tours   AD, D: Philippe Apeloig   DF, SB: Studio Apeloig

Commercial Font ⓕ Galliard / Frutiger

Poster 2003 France   CL: the Museum of Beaux-Arts of Tours   AD, DF, SB: Studio Apeloig   D: Philippe Apeloig

ABCDEFGHIJKLMNOPQRSTUVWXYZ abcdefghijklmnoparstuvwxyz

Custom Font   TM font   http://www.tm-online.nl

Poster 2004 Netherlands   CL: KVGO Amsterdam   AD, D, SB: Richard Niessen

■ 1102 BA Amsterdam ZO ■ The Netherlands ■
TM ■ Florijn 34 a

Custom Font ■ TM font ⬇ http://www.tm-online.nl

Stationary Envelope 2003 Netherlands CL: TM AD, D, SB: Richard Niessen

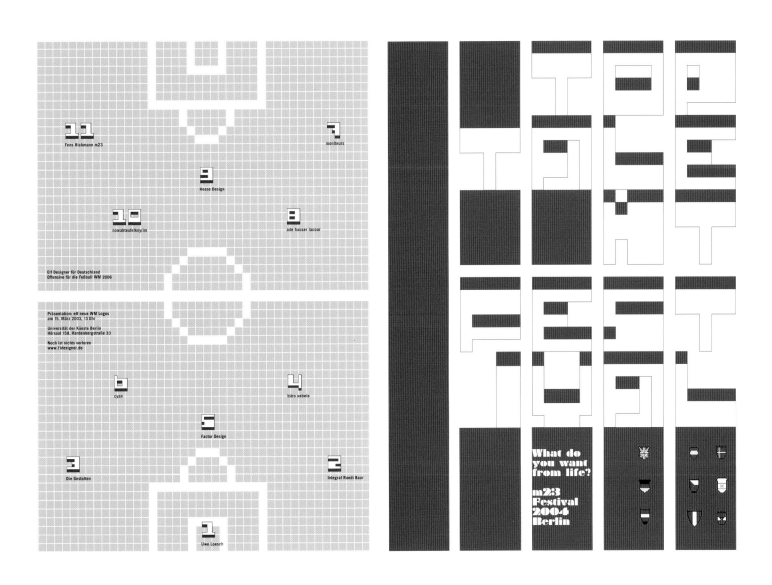

newagimembers2000jonathanbarnbrook
(uk)heribertbirnbach(germany)günte
rkarlbose(germany)marioneuchars(u
k)sarafanelli(uk)isidroferrer(spai
n)detleffiedleranddanielahaufe(ger
many)reinhardgassner(austria)julia
hasting(usa)bradholland(usa)mirkoi
lić(usa)björnkusoffsky(sweden)mich
aelmabry(usa)johnmaeda(usa)pabloma
rtín(spain)richardmcguire(usa)phil
lippemillot(france)etiennemineur(f
rance)petermoser(switzerland)chens
haohua(china)leonardosonnoli(italy
)jennifersterling(usa)swipstolk(ne
therlands)yurisurkoff(russia)marti
nwoodtli(switzerland)wangxu(china)

ABCDEFGHIJKLMNOPQRSTUVWXYZ abcdefghijklmnopqrstuvwxyz
ABCDEFGHIJKLMNOPQRSTUVWXYZ ABCDEFGHIJKLMNOPQRSTUVWXYZ
ABCDEFGHIJKLMNOPQRSTUVWXYZ abcdefghijklmnopqrstuvwxyz

Custom Font   ■ Myrna Regular / Yellow / White
Newsletter 2002 U.S.A.   CL: the Alliance Graphique Internationale (AGI)   CD, AD, D: Gelman   AD: David Heasty   DF, SB: Design Machine

AGIMEXICOCITYCAMINOREALCOCKTAILSSYMPOSIUMstudentsandyoungprof
essionalsoldfactorydiscothequesalon21wernerjeker,o,blechmanky
lecooperchristophniemannkatherineZaskJavierMariscalaudienceve
ningdancinglivebandsintothenightlocalstudentslistening43members
cocktailreceptionlife-sizedpuppetscobblestonestreetspaperlantern
passcourtyardcaminorealoldcloisterchapelthursdayfernandosolan
adesigninthepastconfradofostadomadeinmexicomariscalustrinoma
debutterpizzaromeroarchitecturemexicantalkphilosophiesheadp
honesttranslationechoesbouncingchapelwallslanguagesafternoonbus
esmontrealbansizescalehistoryruinslayeredpyramidsdinnermuseumo
fcontemporaryartmusicconcoctionsmexicanchefsconcludedmealplaza
shotsmezcaltequilahollowbamboeveninginvitationsgovernorsmans
ionfolkloremexicanatraditionalcostumesheadgearsaturdaygeneral
lassemblyclinedupbehindtablesleustedstairstepscalledfooraders
lexanderforadanonkneescrossinghimselfaskingforabsolutionkenvoice
echoingreportingtasksfinanceseducationarchivepublicationsnewme
mberupcomingcongressparispierrebernardlaurencemadarelienextye
arf50thanniversaryagiparis,franceoctober2001fridaymorningvideo
foodaryraesiTinmotionvisualdosanchezperfectlylocal,perfectlyglob
l,performancejesusayounglaiescostumessongtheaterinventionsleon
ardodavinciusesteotilandavalleuillatexsurfeancientchurchfirst
treesgroundfestyrugraesignedbymemberswovenbyvillagerssweek
sperrug1,5kilometerspeechesbandschildarenritualsfeatherdancelaters
ponsor:magujouisualproductstechnologytransformsspacebuilding
sbusesfakarms"henry"ruedruedr20yearsassecretarysteppingdown
rued;,jeanrobert,uweloesch,steffeissbuhlernewkencato,daviahill
man,niklaustroxler,finalpartyankodominoculturalcenterforxxca
atheredcourtyardamericandesignprojectedthrownonfacades,niche
s,columns,monumentstypecolorimagescuervotequilasueandjimterry
acefullmoonlankernwatermelonscrabsparadingbehindthatpuppets
12to15feethighbambooissuepaperwoodenbullsbullfightschargingro
cketsfireworksspewingwhirlingdancingbouncingfTnakingburningfisi
ngfirecrackersclimbingfxfr2000laterhotelsbeds,morningleftcountry

AGIPARISMON249:30IECMEETING13:00LUNCH14:30IECME
ETING19:30DRINKSANDDINNERTUE259:30NEWMEMBERSSE
LECTION13:00LUNCH14:30NEWMEMBERSSELECTION19:30B
IBLIOTHEQUEFORNEWSAVIGNACEXHIBITIONWELCOMEDRIN
KSWED269:30CENTREPOMPIDOUSEMINARINSEARCHOFEXCE
LLENCESPEAKERS:IRMABOOMWERNERJEKERJOHNMAEDAAB
BOTTMILLER13:00LUNCH14:30PEDROPERETGUNTERRAMBO
WKOICHISATO19:30FIESTADANCEOPENFORNONMEMBERST
HU279:30BIBLIOTHEQUENATIONALEDEFRANCEWELCOMETH
EKEYSOFTHECITY50YEARSOFAGIVIDEORUEDIBAURPETERKN
APPRUDIMEYER13:000PENINGEXHIBITION:LEGRAPHISMED
ANSTOUSSESETATS14:30FREE:ARCHITECTURALWALKSETC.
19:30BATEAU-MOUCHEONTHESEINEDINNERPERFORMANCEF
RI289:30CONGRESSZAPPINGPIPPOLIONNIMADEBYCHILDR
ENALAINLEQUERNECSTUDENTS13:00LUNCH14:30FREE17:30
OPENINGANDDRINKS:ANATOMEGALLERYEXHIBITIONPARIS
SEENBY19:30HOTELDESULLYDINNERSHOWLESEXTINCTEURS
SAT299:30CONGRESSGENERALASSEMBLYNEWMEMBERSAGI
ANDTHEFUTURERESULTSPROJECTIONS@M13:00LUNCH14:30
FREE19:30GREATBALLMUSEEFORAINSUN309:30DEPARTURE

オプ・トランス！
OP-trance!

CURATED BY SAWARAGI NOI × AZUMAYA TAKASHI

UKAWA NAOHIRO
ITO ATSUHIRO
HIGASHIONNA YUICHI
MURAYAMA RURIKO
IZUMI KIYOSHI
SATO ISAO

2001.06.16 SAT - 07.29 SUN

KPOキリンプラザ大阪　KIRIN PLAZA OSAKA

Custom Font　☒ Custom made for this project
Flyer 2001 Japan   CL: KIRIN PLAZA OSAKA   AD: Naoki Sato   DF, SB: ASYL DESIGN

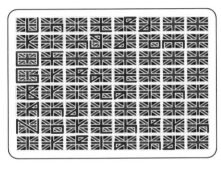

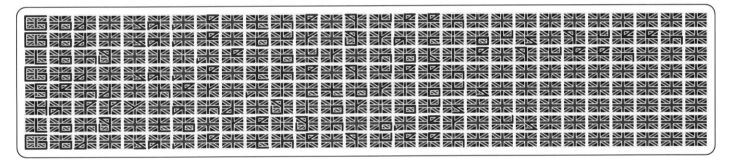

p145

Custom Font | Union Jack

Original Works 2002 Japan   AD, D, DF, SB: dainippon type organization

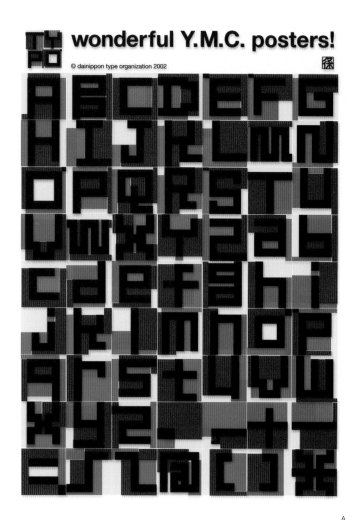

A

B

Commercial Font　YMC alphabet Yellow / YMC alphabet Magenta / YMC alphabet Cyan

Poster　2002　Japan　AD, D, DF, SB: dainippon type organization

wonderful Y.M.C. posters!

© dainippon type organization 2002

C

wonderful Y.M.C. posters!

© dainippon type organization 2002

D

The poster of the concept that it will be set to A if B-D is piled up.

B-Dを重ね合わせるとAになるというコンセプトのポスター。

Poster

ABCDEFGHIJKLMNOPQRSTUVWXYZ

ABCDEFGHIJKLMNOPQRSTUVWXYZ abcdefghijklmnopqrstuvwxyz

Commercial Font · LINETO BIFF / LINETO AKKURAT BOLD · http://www.lineto.com/

Poster, Direct Mail 2004 Switzerland CL: MUSEUM FÜR GESTALTUNG ZÜRICH D, SB: Cornel Windlin TY (BIFF): REALA TY (AKKURAT): Laurenz Brunner P: Isabel Truniger

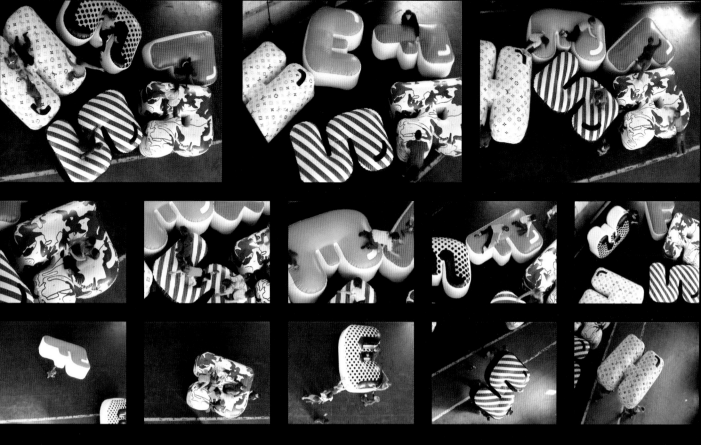

04. MAI, 20 UHR – «Umbruch», Dokumentarfilm von Hans-Ulrich Schlumpf, Schweiz 1987. «Um

26. MAI, 19 UHR – Buchvernissage «Frische Schriften/Fresh Type» und Gesprächsrunde «Schrift transportiert alles!». Mit André Baldinger, Grafiker, Lausanne/Paris; Marco Walser, Visueller Gestalter, Elektrosmog, Zürich; Reinhard Binder, Chief Creative Officer, Interbrand Zintzmeyer & Lux, Berlin/Zürich; Viktor Stampfli, Grafiker, Kommission für Strassen-signalisation, Winikon. Moderation: Andres Janser, Kurator Museum für Gestaltung Zürich. Veranstaltet in Zusammen-arbeit mit dem Haus Konstruktiv. Buchvernissage «Frische

15. JUNI, 20 UHR – «Handschrift und Charakter. Schrift und Corporate Design für Siemens». Vortrag von Hans-Jürg Hunziker, Typograf, Auxerre, und Jürgen Barthel, Director of Communications, Siemens, München.

27. APRIL – Andres Janser, Kurator Museum für
04. MAI – Hans-Rudolf Bosshard, Typograf, Züri
11. MAI – Christoph Bignens, Kunsthistoriker, Zürich
18. MAI – Andres Janser, Kurator Museum für Gestaltung
25. MAI – François Rappo, Grafiker, Ecal, Lausanne. François R
01. JUNI – Gilles Gavillet & David Rust, Grafiker, Optimo, Lausanne. Gille
08. JUNI – Agnès Laube, Grafikerin, Zürich. Agnès Laube, Grafikerin, Zürich. Agn
15. JUNI – Christian Brändle, Direktor Museum für Gestaltung Zürich. Christian Brändle, Dir
22. JUNI – Christoph Bignens, Kunsthistoriker, Zürich. Christoph Bignens, Kunsthistoriker, Zürich. Chris
29. JUNI – Hans-Rudolf Bosshard, Typograf, Zürich. Hans-Rudolf Bosshard, Typograf, Zürich. Hans-Rudolf Bosshard, Typo

Spezialführungen auf Anfrage: doris.bram@hgka.ch oder Telefon 043 446 67 12. Spezialführungen auf Anfrage: doris.bram@hgka.ch oder Telefon

Fr isc he
Sch rif ten
21 04 2004 – 04 07 2004

MUSEUM FÜR GESTALTUNG ZÜRICH

NEUE SCHRIFTEN ENTSTEHEN derzeit in grosser Zahl – für Bücher, Drucksachen, Bildschirme, Strassentafeln. Auch manche Firma setzt auf Schrift als Corporate Design. Den Anstoss zu dieser Blüte gab der Computer, mit dem sich

BUCHSTABEN EINFACHER konstruieren lassen. Nun stehen den zurück-haltenden Alphabeten, die dem lesenden Auge Form und Rhythmus bieten wollen, betont spielerische Schriften gegenüber, die aus Alltagsgegen-ständen «gebaut» oder bis an die Grenze der Lesbarkeit verformt sind.

DIE AUSSTELLUNG ZEIGT Arbeiten von André Baldinger, Ludovic Balland/The Remingtons, Rudolf Barmettler, Laurent Benner, Laurenz Brunner, Büro Destruct, Elektrosmog, Hansjakob Fehr, Gilles Gavillet/Optimo, Sibylle Hagmann, Hektor, Hans-Jürg Hunziker, Intégral Ruedi Baur, Jürg Lehni, Urs Lehni & Rafael Koch, Lineto, Bruno Maag, Hans-Eduard Meier, Stephan Pronto Müller, Norm, PingPong, François Rappo, Mathias Schweizer, Nico Schweizer, Philipp Stamm, Verband der Strassen- und Verkehrs-fachleute, Cornel Windlin und Martin Woodtli.

Custom Font   OCRF (FontFont) customized to monospaced

Poster 2002 Netherlands   CL: Yale University School of Art   AD, D: Min Choi   DF, SB: Sulki & Min Choi

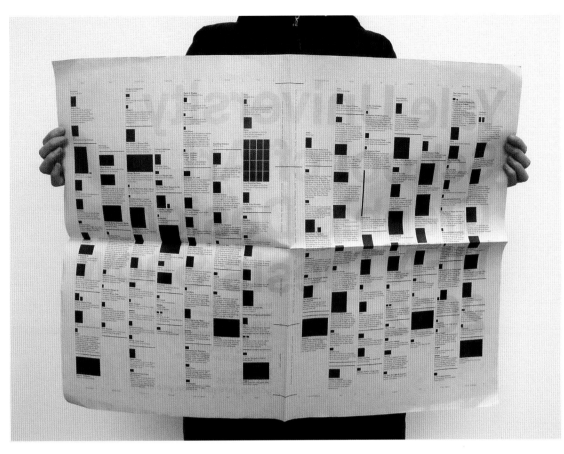

Commercial Font   ⬛F Helvetica / Century School Book / Politie

Poster, Invitation 2002 Netherlands   CL: Yale University School of Art   AD, D: Min Choi   DF, SB: Sulki & Min Choi

 **KANSALLISTEATTERI**

```
*********************************************
```
Hella Wuolijoki /

NISKAVUOREN NUORI EMÄNTÄ

```
*********************************************
```
ensi-ilta 17.12.04 /
Suuri näyttämö

```
*********************************************
```
ohjaus /
Juha Lehtola

koreografia /
Matti Paloniemi

musiikki /
Maria Kalaniemi

lavastus ja puvut /
Kristiina Saha

```
*********************************************
```
rooleissa /
Wanda Dubiel, Marjukka Halttunen, Olli Ikonen,
Markku Maalismaa, Minttu Mustakallio, Heikki
Nousiainen, Anna Paavilainen (TeaK), Ilja
Peltonen, Sari Puumalainen, Katja Salminen,
Hanna Korhonen, Anna Paavilainen, Sami Paasila,
Reetta Pirhonen, Timo Saari

```
*********************************************
```
www.kansallisteatteri.fi

Custom Font   ▉ Custom made for this project / Magda
Poster 2004 Finland   CL: Finnish National Theatre   AD, D, I: Teemu Suviala   AD, I: Antti Hinkula   P: Matti Pyykkö   DF, SB: Syrup Helsinki

Custom Font **F** DECIO 100 CRIS@BREAD-AND-BUTTER.CH
Poster 2003 Switzerland CL: PROJECT FOR FETE DE LA MUSIQUE, LAUSANNE AD: Cristina Bolli-Freitas D: Gael Paccard I: Cristina and Gael P: Laurent Bolli DF, SB: bread and butter, bolli and partner

Custom Font **F** LE RAPPO CRIS@BREAD-AND-BUTTER.CH
Poster 2003 Switzerland CL: FETE DE LA MUSIQUE, LAUSANNE AD: Cristina Bolli-Freitas D: Gael Paccard I: Cristina and Gael P: Lay-out using pictures from Bettina Komeda (THE FACE vol.3, no.7) and Gael Paccard. DF, SB: bread and butter, bolli and partner

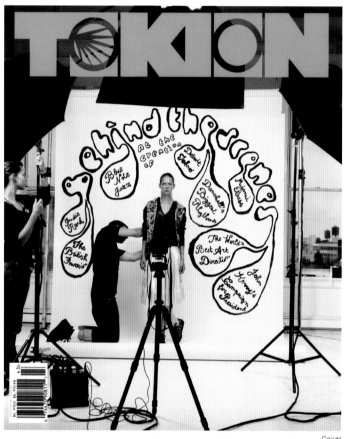

Cover

Others   All untitled custom design fonts by Deanne Cheuk

Magazine 2004 U.S.A.   CL: Tokion Magazine   AD, D, I, SB: Deanne Cheuk   P (Cover): Stefan Ruiz

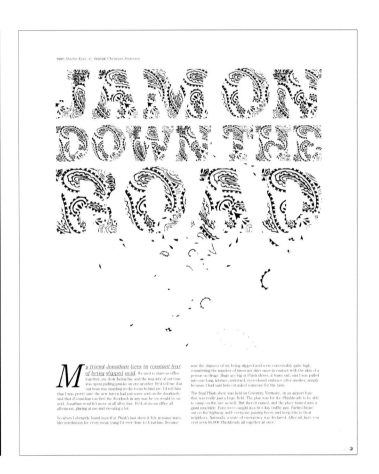

Who is it that makes a great album? The obvious answer is the artist in the studio and later performing the hits onstage. But in the background are the men at the controls, the producers and engineers who help shape and realize the performer's vision, and the records they have recorded rank as some of the best of all time: *A Love Supreme, My Generation, Exile On Mainstreet, Marquee Moon, Heroes, Fear of a Black Planet, Surfer Rosa* and many more. They may not be household names but their legacy will live on, etched in vinyl long after the spotlight fades.

TEXT: *Starlee King* & PHOTOS: *Christian Patterson*

My friend *Jonathan* lives in *constant fear of being slipped acid*. We used to share an office together, my desk facing his, and the majority of our time was spent pulling pranks on one another. He'd tell him that I was pretty sure the new intern had put some acid on the doorknob, and that if Jonathan touched the doorknob in any way he'd be too would be on acid. Jonathan wouldn't move at all after that. He'd sit in our office all afternoon, glaring at me and sweating a lot.

So when I abruptly found myself at Phish's last show it felt, in many ways, like retribution for every mean thing I'd ever done to Jonathan. Because

now the chances of my being slipped acid were conceivably quite high, considering the number of times my skin came in contact with the skin of a person on drugs. Hugs are big at Phish shows, it turns out, and I was pulled into one long, intense, awkward, eyes-closed embrace after another, simply because I had said hello or asked someone for the time.

The final Phish show was held in Coventry, Vermont, on an airport base that was really just a huge field. The plan was for the Phishheads to be able to camp on the site as well. But then it rained, and the place turned into a giant mudslide. Fans were caught in a two-day traffic jam. Parties broke out on the highway, with everyone passing beers and being fits to their neighbors. Naturally, a state of emergency was declared. After all, have you ever seen 60,000 Phishheads all together at once?

TEXT: *Daisuke Nakimura* ⋅ PHOTO: *Ryusuke Saito*

YAMATAKA EYE

When Yamataka Eye first started making music in the legendary noise outfit Hanatarash, he was known to use everything from a chainsaw to firecrackers as instruments. Though his subsequent band, the Boredoms, managed to gain a cross-over audience in the U.S. thanks to a slew of high profile admirers, Eye has never wavered from his adventurous approach to music. Which, as he will tell you, is the same thing as having an adventurous approach to life itself.

What kind of music did you listen to when you formed the Boredoms?
Yamataka Eye: I was doing tape recording – I mean so-called 'home recordings.' I wanted to do a rock band, but there were no people who could do it with me. Nobody was listening to punk or New Wave, so I reluctantly formed an imaginary band, 'The Boredoms.' I took the name from the song 'Boredom' by the Buzzcocks. My life was a boring one, so I picked it up. That was a long time ago - nearly ten or twenty years ago, because I've been doing this since 1986.

How has the Boredoms' music changed over the years?
YE: There's been no change. It's still acid punk.

Early in your career you mostly played in New York, right?
YE: (Jazz musician) John Zorn was the first person to call me to come play America, and he invited me to go on tour. We traveled with a grindcore band called Brutal Truth – at the time, Earache (Records) was quite popular, and we loved those bands. So I did *Naked City* with John, which was like a mixture of hardcore, cut-up free jazz and various film scores, and we would change styles very quickly. It was quite complicated – there would be an element of grind, and after that film music would join in for a bit and then silence and then a blast of noise. It was really extreme, but finally Earache decided to publish it. The members of Brutal Truth are from New York, and they joined in while I was doing sessions with John, and we became friendly.

How was it for the Boredoms to play Lollapalooza? It seems like that might be a difficult crowd for you...
YE: No, I really enjoyed it, because the first show was at Las Vegas. It was really hot, and the place has absolutely no spirituality. I thought that was amazing – being so *nothing*.

The Boredoms have had a lot of drummers and percussionists. What is the role of percussion in your sound?
YE: Percussion is very important. Banging and knocking is really important, like making percussive noise or vibrations, even while you're walking and that sort of thing. Knocking against something itself is important, because it's an ordinary action. Maybe it has to do with touching or verifying, but those kinds of cutaneous sensations are important. Drums were made with human skin and played by bones in the ancient era. It seems brutal, but if you bang skin with bones, it improves blood circulation. Something happens, like the improvement of the flow of energy. That kind of feeling means a lot to me.

Why did it take so long for the Boredoms to make a new album?
YE: Well, we're now making music only with drums, and since we were in this period of transition, it made us have to think about what we were doing more. But we were also neglectful and lazy. Yes, we were recording, but we were just doing it without worrying about the outcome. When we started collecting up those recordings, we needed to concentrate, like verifying the evidence. So we didn't hurry with these pieces...

Do you think everything can be music?
YE: I think so. Everything can be resolved into music or vibration – anything and everything. Everything exists with its specific vibration – like, its character or nature. That nature has nothing to do with the problems of men or women, but simply means our existence. It is a vibration, and it also can be some kind of music. So, in that sense, if we see everything as vibrations, all things can be music. Even the universe.

Are you friends with a lot of other noise musicians?
YE: Not many, but I know K. K. Null, who played with Merzbow.

Are you close to Merzbow?
YE: He was the first man that I got interested in when I started a band. I had never been to Tokyo, and when I'd think about who I wanted to meet in Tokyo - Akita Masami (AKA 'Merzbow.')

TEXT: *Ken Miller* ⋅ PHOTO: *Alex Freund*

YOKO ONO

I try to give instructions that are encouraging and inspiring. Especially nowadays, you need that.

BLUE SUN DAY

Photography by PETER STANGLMAYR

Stylist: Jay Massacret / Hair: Ramona @ Bumble & Bumble / Makeup: Yuka Washizu for Dior / Models: Brian @ Request, Gordon @ IMG

SpringSummer 05 preview

GORDON wears shirts by OPENING CEREMONY, wears jacket by ISSEY MIYAKE and vest by CLOAK

Yao Ming is 7'6" tall, which means he looks pretty funny when you sit him next to Mini Me on an airplane. Yao Ming is also the only basketball player from China to have been drafted first in the NBA draft, which means he has become an instant superstar, selling out arenas wherever he goes and attracting crowds on the street. Yao Ming also has the expectations of an entire country (a really, really big country) to shoulder, with his every move scrutinized as a source of shame or pride. We spoke to him through an interpreter and tried to gain a little perspective on his adjustment to life as a celebrity in a new country.

YOU COME FROM A FAMILY OF BASKETBALL PLAYERS – WAS IT ALWAYS ASSUMED THAT YOU WOULD PLAY, TOO?

YAO MING: My parents actually wanted me to go to school and do something more academic with my life, but I just love the sport so much that I stuck with it since my youth. I ended up making the National Team and the Shanghai Sharks, and I knew then that basketball would be a successful career for me.

CAN YOU TELL US A BIT ABOUT YOUR EARLY DAYS PLAYING BASKETBALL?

YM: I received my first formal basketball training when I joined the Youth Sports School at age nine. I was then selected to the Shanghai Youth Team at age 14. By then I was out of the house and living with my teammates. As basketball players in China, we always live with our teammates in an area that is adjacent to the basketball arenas. Our coaches and the administration always made sure that our diet was very good, and we had to go to bed at a certain hour, so the lights would go out at that time. Even though we had strict living conditions, I felt that

Though he left school with only an eighth grade education, Mat Hoffman has demonstrated his command of the scientific method by conducting a highly complex series of tests on his own body. His thesis—that he is one of the most creative, fearless, resilient individuals among us today—has been amply proven. Moreover, he has shown a remarkable understanding of gravity, whether launching his BMX bike to unforeseen heights, jumping off buildings or rocketing at ridiculous speeds out of an airplane.

FIRST THINGS FIRST, WHAT'S YOUR INJURY/SURGERY COUNT UP TO THESE DAYS?

MAT HOFFMAN: I don't know, man. I stopped counting. I've broken over 50 bones. I just had a surgery earlier this year, and it was my 13th operation. I'm down to duct tape and zip ties now.

KEEPING YOUR COSTS DOWN?

MH: Ahh no. Most of the surgeries have been for knee stuff and shoulder stuff. Now I'm doing operations that aren't sanctioned by the FDA. I found this doctor in Dijon, France, and they make a ligament which is a synthetic ACL. I had (already) gone through an ACL from a cadaver, and I just broke my shoulder so many times that I stared looking at options like that. I started joking with my doctor about finding one made out of a bike chain. They can't do too much because its not sanctioned, and they could loose their license, so I did my own research and found some stuff. I've been putting my body back together with some of the great medical science out there.

DO YOU HAVE HEALTH INSURANCE THESE DAYS?

MH: Yeah, well... my insurance company dropped me because I've been hurt so much. I was self-insured for about three years, and it was just killing me, so I made cameos in a couple of movies last year to get on SAG. I have insurance through them now. It works good, too, because they obviously know that stuntmen are going to get jacked up, so they're a little more tolerant of my behavior.

ARE YOU SURPRISED TO BE ALIVE?

MH: Yeah, I never looked too far into the future. When you do a lot of the stuff I love doing, you can't think about it too much. Your mind kind of gets in the way because it draws the limits for you, so you have to live through instinct. Your soul and spirit carry you, and you let your instinct respond to it. You can discover so much more stuff that way, you know. I've always lived like that. Looking back, I'm definitely living on extra credit.

WHAT KEEPS YOU GOING?

MH: There are so many things you can do that people don't know about. I don't just do things without evaluating the dangers of it. (I don't) just throw some dice and hope I make it through. But I do let myself

Photographer **KT Auleta**
Stylist **Jay Massacret**
Hair **John Ruidant** @ See Management
Models **Brian & Jordan** both @ Request
Thanks to Jabari Gaariti from Thornton W. Burgess middle school, Hampden, MA

Brian wears sweatpants by **Umbro Contrast** and t-shirt by **Kim Jones** / **Jordan** wears sweatpants by **Umbro Contrast** and jacket by **Kim Jones**

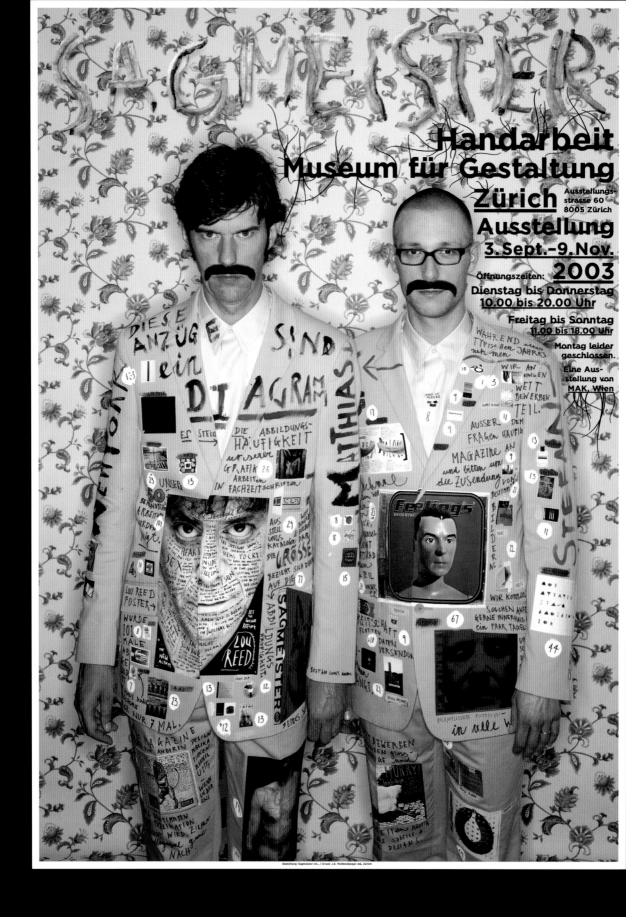

Poster 2003 U.S.A. CL: Museum für Gestaltung Zürich AD, D: Stefan Sagmeister D: Matthias Ernstberger P: Bela Borsodi DF, SB: Sagmeister Inc.

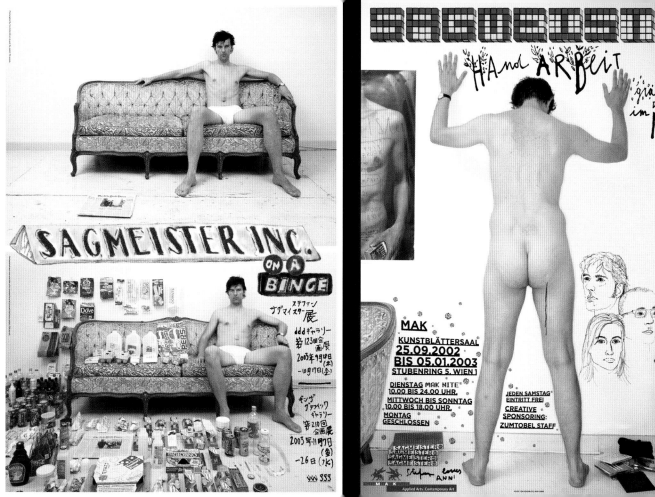

Magazine Spreads 2002 U.S.A. CL: .copy magazine AD, D: Stefan Sagmeister D, Model Making: Eva Hueckmann D, P: Matthias Ernstberger D: Doris Pesendorfer Backgrounds (everything, to me): Wolf-Gordon Inc. DF, SB: Sagmeister hc.

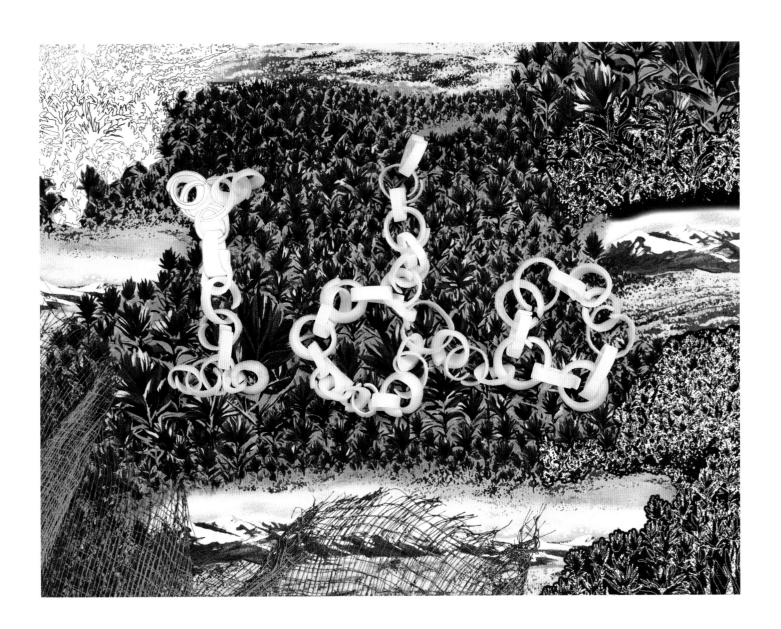

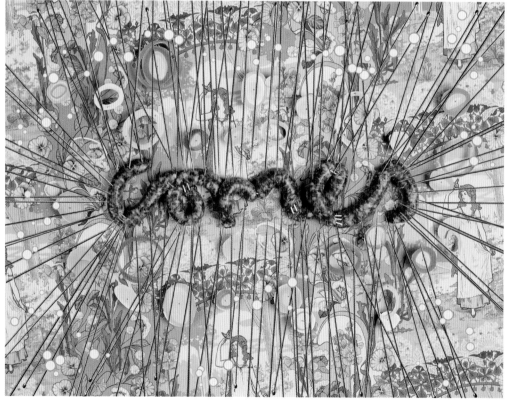

>>> Continued from the previous page.

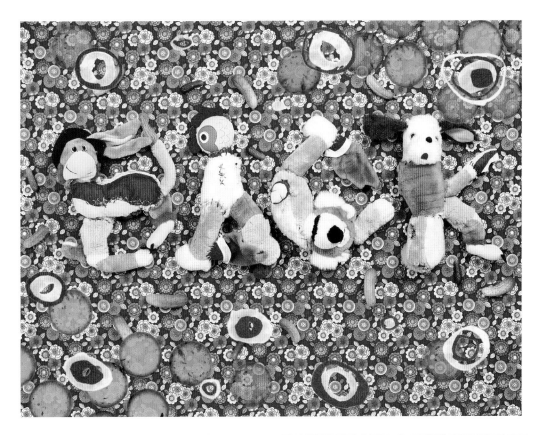

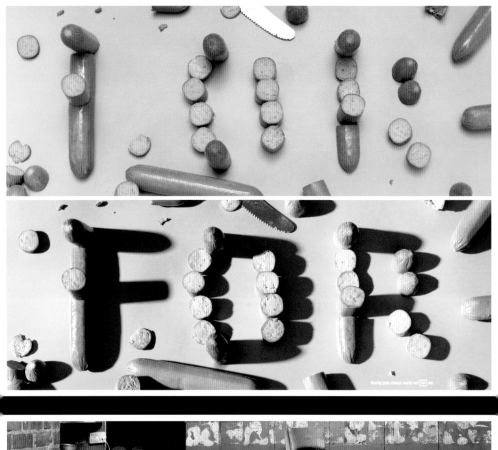

Having guts always works out for me.

Having guts always works out for me.

```
                TARGET
             3728 Route 22
              Union NJ
             732.882.7438


    Ticket#383578 Cus#WALK-IN      Dec 21 02
    Usr NS    Slp HOU Rg# 15 Dr# 10   Time 02:1
    ------------------------------------------------

    Item Number      Qty     Price    Ext

    321063            1      85.99    85.99
    NIKE AIR RIFFS
                            ========================
    SUBTOTAL                            85.99
    TAX                                  7.84
                            ========================
    TOTAL                               93.83


              LUI, FUNGJIAE


              3333333333
           333333333333333333
          333333333333333333333
         6333333333333333333333333
         33333333333333 3333333333333
        7333333333        2333333333
        3333333            3333333
       3333333              23333333333
       333332     632      33333333333
       333336    3333      33333 63333
       333336           66    2333333
       333333     337333333   33333333
      33333333   33337233333733333333
      3333333336   37 22333 33333333
     333333333333336   2633333333333
   33333333333333333337 3333333333333333
   333333333333333333   7333333333333333
   333333333333333333333333333333333333333
   333333333333333333333333333333333333333
   333333333333333333333333333333333333333
   333333333333333333333333333333333333333
   333333333333333333333333333333333333333
   333333333333333333333333333333333333333
   333333333333333333333333333333333333333
   333333333333333333333333333333333333333
   333333333333333333333333333333333333333
   333333333333333333333333333333333333333
   333333333333333333333333333333333333333
   333333333333333333333333333333333333333
   333333333333333333333333333333333333333
   333333333333333333333333333333333333333


   ***********************************************
   * WORKER                                      *
   ***********************************************
   5612: AGE:19
   LUI, FUNGJIAE

   ***********************************************
   * FACTORY                                     *
   ***********************************************
   SEWON FACTORY
   JIAOZHOU, SHANDONG, CHINA

   ***********************************************
   * WORKING HOUR                                *
   ***********************************************
   10 HOURS PER DAY
   6 DAYS PER WEEK

   ***********************************************
   * WORKER WAGE                                 *
   ***********************************************
   35 YUAN PER DAY
   3.70 US DOLLARS

   ***********************************************
   * MINIMUM WAGE IN MEXICO                      *
   ***********************************************
   45 YUAN PER DAY
   4.75 US DOLLARS

   ***********************************************
   * 500 MG OF RICE IN CHINA                     *
   ***********************************************
   10 YUAN
   1 US DOLLARS

   ***********************************************
   * AVERAGE COST TO FEED FAMILY OF FOUR         *
   ***********************************************
   140 YUAN A DAY
   14 US DOLLARS

   SOURCE INFORMATION
   WWW.SWEATSHOPWATCH.ORG
   WWW.WORKERSIGHT.ORG
   ILO.ORG


         ** HAVE A NICE DAY **
```

```
                TARGET
             3728 Route 22
              Union NJ
             732.882.7438


    Ticket#383578 Cus#WALK-IN      Dec 21 02
    Usr NS    Slp HOU Rg# 15 Dr# 10   Time 02:1
    ------------------------------------------------

    Item Number      Qty     Price    Ext

    JS0089-2          3      99.83   199.49
    NIKE AIR RIFFS
                            ========================
    SUBTOTAL                           199.49
    TAX                                 17.02
                            ========================
    TOTAL                              216.51


              HANZOU, CHINA


                       33333
                    333   3333
        333333      333    3333
      3333   333    33333    33
     3333     333   3333      333
    3333   33333333333    33 333
    333                  333333
    33                   33333
    33                    333
   3333              *   33
     333   333           33
      3333333 333        333
          33          33
          33 33333  33333
             33333
```

```
   ***********************************************
   * FACTORY                                     *
   ***********************************************
   SE WON INTERNATIONAL
   JIAO ZHOU, SHANDONG, CHINA

   ***********************************************
   * WORKER                                      *
   ***********************************************
   1156
   CHANG, JUREMO

   ***********************************************
   * WORKING HOUR                                *
   ***********************************************
   10 HOURS PER DAY
   6 DAYS PER WEEK

   ***********************************************
   * WORKER WAGE                                 *
   ***********************************************
   35 YUAN PER DAY
   3.70 US DOLLARS

   ***********************************************
   * MINIMUM WAGE IN MEXICO                      *
   ***********************************************
   45 YUAN PER DAY
   4.75 US DOLLARS

   ***********************************************
   * 500 MG OF RICE IN CHINA                     *
   ***********************************************
   10 YUAN
   1 US DOLLARS

   ***********************************************
   * AVERAGE COST TO FEED FAMILY OF FOUR         *
   ***********************************************
   140 YUAN A DAY
   14 US DOLLARS

   SOURCE INFORMATION
   WWW.SWEATSHOPWATCH.ORG
   WWW.WORKERSIGHT.ORG
   ILO.ORG


         * HAVE A NICE DAY *
```

Commercial Font   **F** BubbledotICG   ⬇ Adobe

Receipt design proposal   2003 Netherlands   CL: Class Work   AD, D: Sulki Choi (collaboration with Jean Servaas)   DF, SB: Sulki & Min Choi

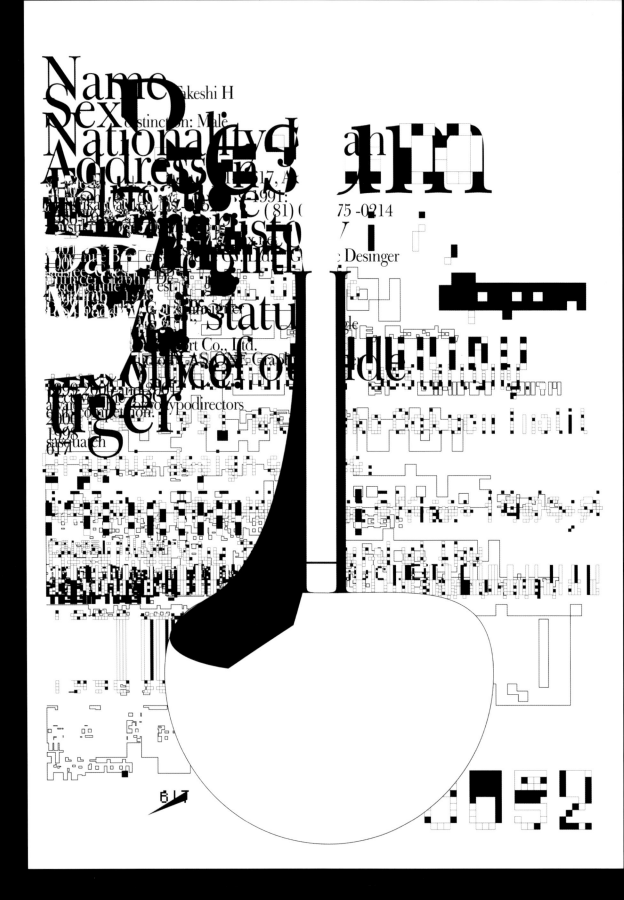

Others   **F** Hand Collage

Page Contribution for Magazine   2004   Japan   CL: FIRCIVE   AD, D, SB: Takeshi Hamada   P: Yuko Imamura   Hair Make: HAMA (A.C.O)   Make: Michiko Funabiki   Stylist: Kumi Saito (A.C.O)   Model: Jamie Bochert (switch models)

Commercial Font   **F** Zapfino / Bracelet (MONSEN)

Magazine AD   2004   Japan   CL: Garcia Marquez   AD, D, I, SB: Takeshi Hamada   P: Emiko Morizaki (Femme)   Hair Make: HAMA (A.C.O)   Produce: +81

Commercial Font   062aPlotter-Bandzug   http://www.forhomeorofficeuse.com

Catalog 2003 France   CL: Colette   D, DF, SB: VIER5

Smear Campaign

Hair / Kusco-Murphy

Start

Art Director & Graphic Designer
Takeshi Hamada

Photographer
Kazuhiro / Watanabe

Hair & Make-up
Hama (FOR ASIAN CULTURE ORGANIZE)

Model
Joice (GUNN's)

Musician
Let's Get Sick by Mu

Editors
Hitomi Nakamura
Masamune Nagao

Flash Design
Atsushi Fujimaki (NON-GRID, INC.)

Special Thanks : Bin, Tetsuya Goto

Foundation / Christian Dior
Sheer Blush / Christian Dior
Lip Conditioner / Christian Dior
Face Pack / Darphin, Cosme Decorte

Back Next

Commercial Font Garamond (MONSEN) Page Contribution for Magazine 2003 Japan CL: hint fashion magazine AD, D, SB: Takeshi Hamada D (Flash): Atsushi Fujimaki (Non-Grid, Inc.)
P: Kazuhiro/Watanabe Hair Make: HAMA (A.C.O) Model: Joice (Gunn's) Director: Hitomi Nakamura / Masamune Nagao

Front

Back

Custom Font / Free Font | F Transit Bold / Wedgie

Poster, Flyer 2004 Germany   CL: Diakonie   AD, D: Fons Hickmann   D: Barbara Bättig   DF, SB: Fons Hickmann m23

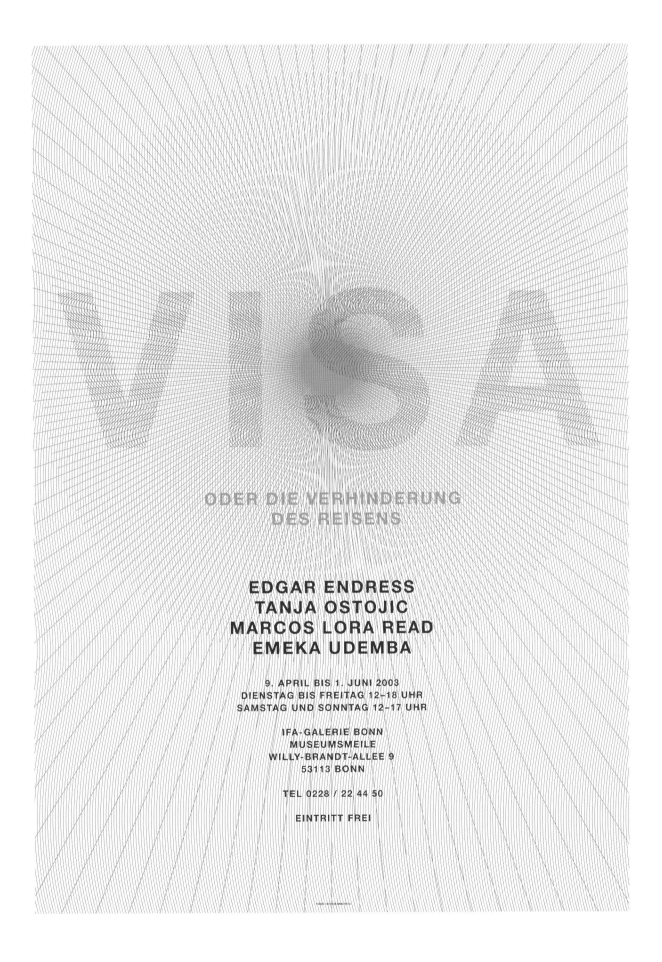

VISA

ODER DIE VERHINDERUNG
DES REISENS

EDGAR ENDRESS
TANJA OSTOJIC
MARCOS LORA READ
EMEKA UDEMBA

9. APRIL BIS 1. JUNI 2003
DIENSTAG BIS FREITAG 12–18 UHR
SAMSTAG UND SONNTAG 12–17 UHR

IFA-GALERIE BONN
MUSEUMSMEILE
WILLY-BRANDT-ALLEE 9
53113 BONN

TEL 0228 / 22 44 50

EINTRITT FREI

Custom Font   **F** Helvetica manipulated

Poster 2004 Germany CL: ifa Art Gallery AD, D: Fons Hickmann AD: Simon Gallus D: Barbara Bättig DF, SB: Fons Hickmann m23

LOGH
sweden
PHOEBUS
support
09. 06. 2004

ZENTRUM *altenberg*
oberhausen
WALZENLAGER
www.konzerteimwalzenlager.de

ABCDEFGHIJKLMNOPQRSTUVWXYZ abcdefghijklmnopqrstuvwxyz
ABCDEFGHIJKLMNOPQRSTUVWXYZ abcdefghijklmnopqrstuvwxyz

Commercial Font CA Geheimagnet-Normal / CA Geheimagnet-BoldItalic http://www.cape-arcona.com
Poster 2004 Germany CL: Zentrum Altenberg AD, D: Stefan Claudius P: Nannette Römer DF, SB: Claudius Design

p132
p133

ABCDEFGHIJKLMNOPQRSTUVWXYZ ABCDEFGHIJKLMNOPQRSTUVWXYZ

ABCDEFGHIJKLMNOPQRSTUVWXYZ abcdefghijklmnopqrstuvwxyz

Commercial Font   **F** Satellite / Wokka   ⬇ http://www.final.nu

Poster 2004 U.S.A. CL: Roots Music Tours AD, D, I, P: Brett Calzada DF, SB: New Emit

ABCDEFGHIJKLMNOPQRSTUVWXYZ abcdefghijklmnopqrstuvwxyz

p142

Commercial Font | CA BND | http://www.cape-arcona.com

Poster 2004 Germany CL: {ths} Design A, D: Thomas Schostok DF, SB: Cape Arcona Type Foundry

ABCDEFGHIJKLMNOPQRSTUVWXYZ abcdefghijklmnopqrstuvwxyz

Commercial Font | ACMc | gunnar@gunnarswanson.com

Poster 1993 U.S.A. CL: The Los Angeles chapter of the American Institute of Graphic Arts AD, D, DF, SB:Gunnar Swanson

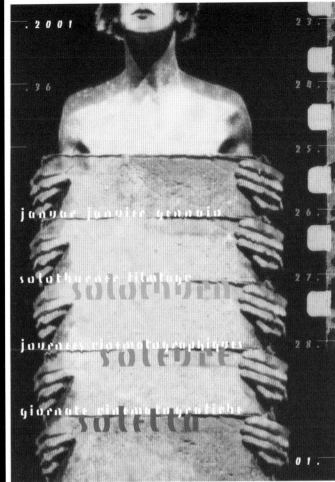

ABCDEFGHIJKLMNOPQRSTUVWXYZ abcdefghijklmnopqrstuvwxyz

Commercial Font   🄵 Jamille Italic   ⤓ http://www.linotype.com

Poster 1998 Switzerland   CL: Silva Neuman, Inflagnanti Boutique   AD, D: Jean-Benoit Lévy   P: Jean-Pascal Imsand   DF, SB: AND (traffic grafic)   Model: Sabina   Photolith: Photolith Sturm AG   Print: Serigraphie Uldry

abcdefghijklmnopqrstuvwxyz

⚲ p148

Custom Font   🄵 Aleph

Poster 2001 Switzerland   CL: Swiss Film Festival   AD, D: Jean-Benoit Lévy   P: Monique Jacot   DF, SB: AND (traffic grafic)   Photolith: Photolitho Sturm AG   Print: Serigraphie Uldry

Commercial Font | **F** written by a typewriter

Poster 2001 France CL, AD, DF, SB: Studio Apeloig D: Philippe Apeloig

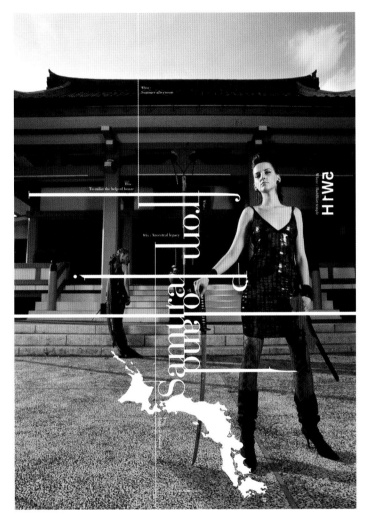

Commercial Font   Akzidenz Grotesk / Neutraface   http://www.bertholdtypes.com/home.html (Akzidenz Grotesk) / http://houseind.com/ (Neutraface)

Poster Art 2004 Japan   CL: Kinmei Printing Co., Ltd.   AD, D: Shun Kawakami   P: Ikuma Yamad / Taisuke Koyama   DF, SB: artless Inc

FILMPODIUM
JULI-AUG.02

Custom Font   ⊞ Custom made for this project / Interstate

Poster 2002 Switzerland   CL: Film-Podium Zürich   D, SB: Ralph Schraivogel   Lithographer: Lithwork   Printer: Serigraphie Uldry

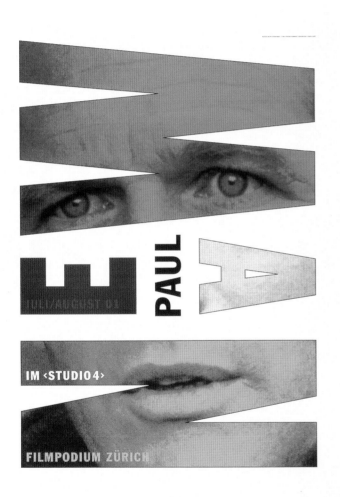

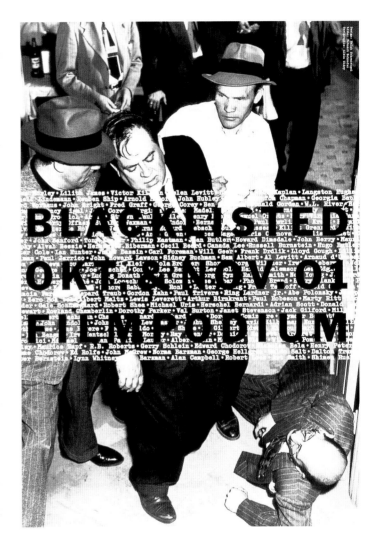

Commercial Font | F Franklin Gothic

Poster 2001 Switzerland CL: Film-Podium Zürich D, SB: Ralph Schraivogel Lithographer: FotoArt Schrofer Printer: Serigraphie Uldry

Commercial Font ⓕ Helvetica

Poster 2001 Switzerland CL: Film-Podium Zürich D, SB: Ralph Schraivogel Lithographer: Egli, Kunz & Partner Printer: Serigraphie Uldry

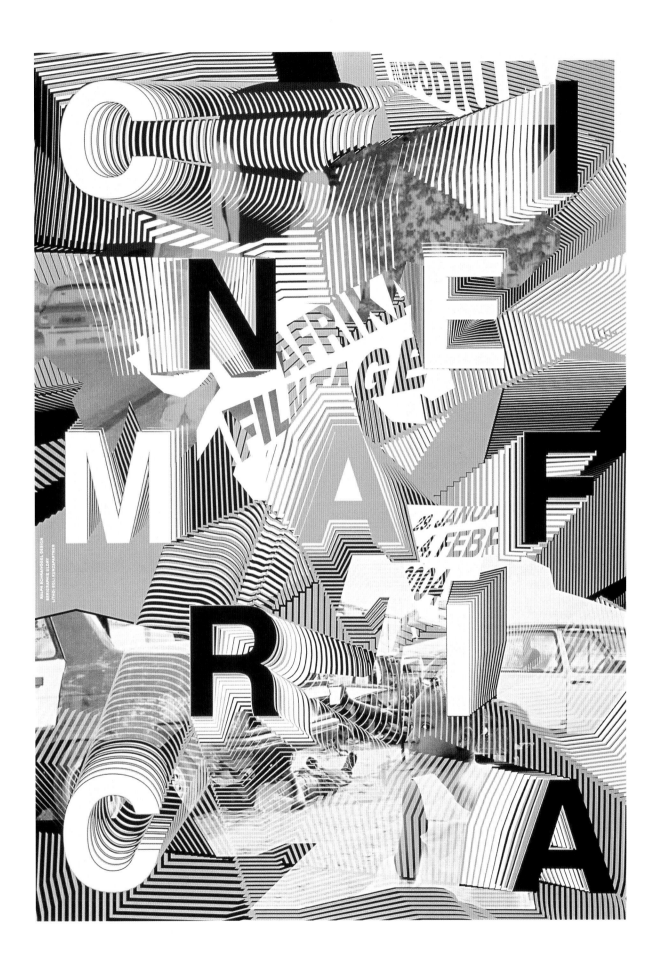

Commercial Font   **F** Helvetica

Poster 2004 Switzerland   CL: Film-Podium Zürich   D, SB: Ralph Schraivogel   Lithographer: Egli, Kunz & Partner   Printer: Serigraphie Uldry

Commercial Font　F Garage

Poster 2003 Switzerland　CL: Organization Puce Aarberg　D, SB: Ralph Schraivogel　Lithographer: Mac　Printer: Serigraphie Uldry

Commercial Font | Univers

Poster 2004 Switzerland   CL: SchaffhausenJazzfestival   D, SB: Ralph Schraivogel   Lithographer: Egli, Kunz & Partner   Printer: Serigraphie Uldry

Commercial Font F Arete Mono / Palantino ↓ http://www.emigre.com

Magazine 2004 Australia, UK CL: Simon Finch Rare Books AD, D: Vince Frost D: Anthony Donovan / Tim Murphy / Matthew Willis DF, SB: emeryfrost / Frost Design

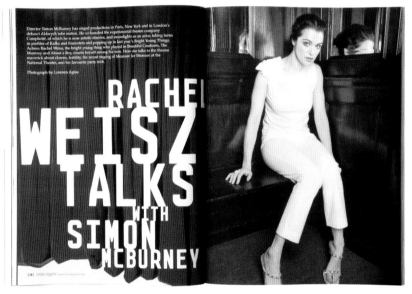

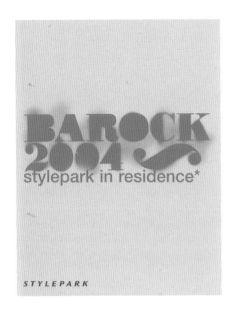

BAROCK 2004
stylepark in residence*

DER THE GLASS
SWAN IN
GLÄSERNE THE
SCHWAN IM
SOZIAL-PALACE
PALAST OF THE
PEOPLE

RALPH NIEMCZYK

SECHS/SIX   SEVEN/SIEBEN

form

THE GOSSIP
SOCIETY DIE
SCHWATZ-
HAFTE GE-
SELLSCHAFT

ZEHN/TEN   ELEVEN/ELF

INTERNI
BAROQUE
ATTITUDE

ZWANZIG/TWENTY   TWENTYONE/EINUNDZWANZIG

ABCDEFGHIJKLMNOPQRSTUVWXYZ abcdefghijklmnopqrstuvwxyz   ♀ p153

Custom Font   🄵 BAROCK (Modified Bodoni) / Helvetica Neue Medium   ⬇ http://www.sign.de

Book 2004 Germany   CL: Stylepark AG   AD, D: Antonia Henschel   P: various   DF, SB: SIGN Kommunikation

VERLAG HERMANN SCHMIDT MAINZ

IN THE OUTSIDE >

SIGN KOMMUNIKATION/
FRANKFURT AM MAIN

2002 >

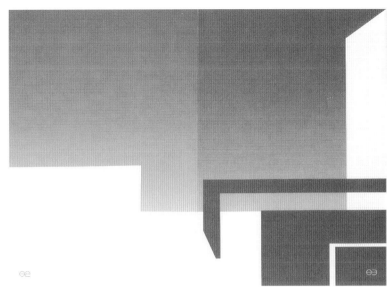

VERLAG HERMANN SCHMIDT MAINZ

ON THE INSIDE >

SIGN KOMMUNIKATION/
FRANKFURT AM MAIN

> 2002

ON THE INSIDE / SIGN KOMMUNIKATION

FONT/SIGN THIN/
SIGN ROUNDED/2001

ON THE INSIDE / SIGN KOMMUNIKATION

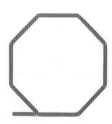

ABCDEFGHIJKLMNOPQRSTUVWXYZ abcdefghijklmnopqrstuvwxyz

| Custom Font | **F** SIGN ROUNDED / Univers http://www.sign.de |

Book 2002 Germany   CL: Verlag Hermann Schmidt Mainz   AD, D, P (On the inside): Antonia Henschel   P (In the outside): Ingmar Kurth   DF, SB: SIGN Kommunikation

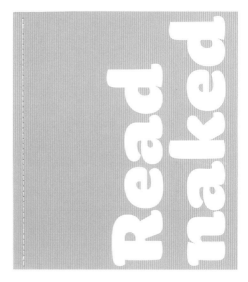

Read naked

IF you have never

been in a sauna and you don't have a clue what a sauna is, don't worry. A sauna is a fairly small room or hut where you enter **naked** and which is heated to **80 degrees** Celcius. You can go in alone or with other people, and everybody sits on a wooden platform close to some really hot stones. These can be heated electrically, but a real fire is much nicer. By **throwing water** on top of the stones, the room fills with **steam**. Within a few minutes you will start to sweat. After a while, you throw another pailful of water on the stones, and you will **sweat** more and more. Beat yourself on your back with a **birch whisk**. This makes your blood circulate, and fills the sauna with a unique smell. After spending some time in there, say around 15 minutes, take a jump into a **lake**. Why all this? We can promise you will feel relaxed. The sauna will clean your body, soothe your mind – in other words, **make you happy**

[8]   [9]

We **used** to sneak into the **hotel** down the road for a swim or a **sauna** and afterwards we all went home commenting on how **good** our skin felt. They have since added proper locks at the **hotel.** Carolina D'Avila (22), a **beauty queen** in Porto Alegre, Brazil.

[10]   [11]

Kurt Weidemann

DESIGNERS' SECRET SAUNA STORIES

TEXT GETS READABLE IN SAUNA (> 80 DEGREES CELSIUS)

[12]   [13]

ABCDEFGHIJKLMNOPQRSTUVWXYZ abcdefghijklmnopqrstuvwxyz

Commercial Font   Sauna   http://www.underware.nl
Book 2002 Finland CL, DF, SB: Underware AD, D: Akiem Helmling / Bas Jacobs / Sami Kortemäki

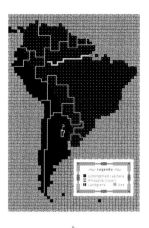

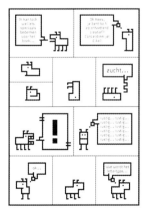

ABCDEFGHIJKLMNOPQRSTUVWXYZ abcdefghijklmnopqrstuvwxyz
ABCDEFGHIJKLMNOPQRSTUVWXYZ abcdefghijklmnopqrstuvwxyz

ABCDEFGHIJKLMNOPQRSTUVWXYZ abcdefghijklmnopqrstuvwxyz

Custom Font   ▪ BOX

Poster 2003 Japan   CL: ACTAR   AD, D, DF, SB: dainippon type organization

p145

A BC DEFGHIJ KLMON PQ RSTUVWXYZ 9b cdefghij klmnopq rstuv w x yz

Custom Font | CUBE

Poster 2003 Japan CL: ACTAR AD, D, DF, SB: dainippon type organization

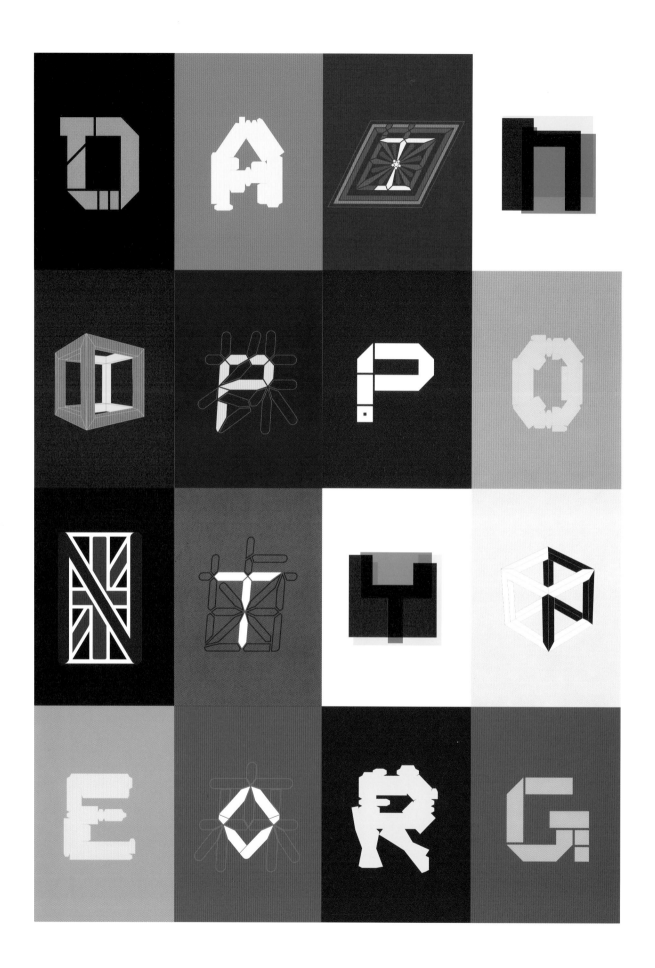

Custom Font   ■ BOX / CUBE / Union Jack / KUROFUNE 20000 / Dentype / TypeStock / Forest / YMC

Flyer   2003   Japan   CL: ACTAR   AD, D, DF, SB: dainippon type organization

Custom Font   Chacao / Chacao3

Poster, Flyer 2003 Venezuela   CL: SIMPL3 Productions   AD, D, I, DF, SB: MASA

Custom Font | tubular / Cachire

Poster, Flyer 2003 Venezuela   CL: SIMPL3 Productions   AD, D, I, DF, SB: MASA

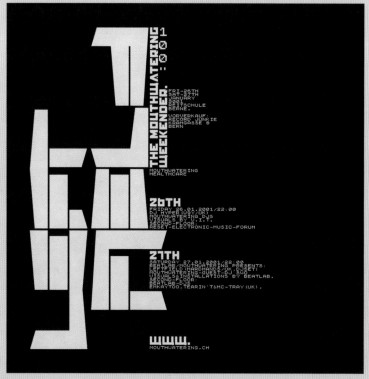

ABCDEFGHIJKLMNOPQRSTUVWXYZ abcdefghijklmnopqrstuvwxyz

p139

Free Font   BD Ramen / Davida   http://www.typedifferent.com

Flyer 2003 Switzerland   CL: Migros, Mouthwatering   D, TY: Lopetz   DF, SB: buro destruct

ABCDEFGHIJKLMNOPQRSTUVWXYZ abcdefghijklmnopqrstuvwxyz

p137

Commercial Font   BD Tatami / Eastbloc / ZX Spectrum   http://www.typedifferent.com

Poster, Flyer 2001 Switzerland   CL: Mouthwatering   D, TY: Lopetz   DF, SB: buro destruct

ABCDEFGHIJKLMNOPQRSTUVWXYZ ABCDEFGHIJKLMNOPQRSTUVWXYZ

p156

| Free Font | BD BDRmono | http://www.typedifferent.com |

Poster, Flyer 1999 Switzerland   CL: Kulturhallen Dampfzentrale Bern   D: MBrunner   TY: Lopetz   DF, SB: buro destruct

p159

| Free Font | BD Alm / Helvetica Neue | http://www.typedifferent.com |

Poster, Flyer 2001 Switzerland   CL: Reitschule Bern   D, TY: Lopetz   DF, SB: buro destruct

ABCDEFGHIJKLMNOPQRSTUVWXYZ abcdefghijklmnopqrstuvwxyz

Custom Font   F Cloud   ⬇ http:www.fellowdesigners.com

Poster 2002 Sweden   CL: Liljevalchs konsthall   AD, D, I: Paul Kühlhorn and Eva Liljefors   DF, SB: Fellow Designers

ABCDEFGHIJKLMNOPQRSTUVWXYZ

Custom Font   ▤ Kajfes   ⬇ http:www.fellowdesigners.com

CD Jacket, Sticker 2004 Sweden CL: Goran Kajfes AD, D, I: Paul Kühlhorn and Eva Liljefors   P: Martin Runeborg / Denise Grünstein   DF, SB: Fellow Designers

SÁBADO 21 DE AGOSTO 2004
AL MODO BAR, LA CASTELLANA 6000BS/CHICAS GRATIS ANTES DE LAS 12
MÚSICA: SPYRO (EN VIVO), LOPEZ VS METRA, WAKE VS CASTOR,
RATA VS HUGE HEFNER, ALEX VS TENZOR, OC VS SHIVER FLAY.
VISUALES: MASA VS TOHYTO, KCHO VS C1RQA, HMTO.

SIMPL3   we ♥ mujeres

SÁBADO 21 DE AGOSTO 2004
AL MODO BAR, LA CASTELLANA 6000BS/CHICAS GRATIS ANTES DE LAS 12
MÚSICA: SPYRO (EN VIVO), LOPEZ VS METRA, WAKE VS CASTOR,
RATA VS HUGE HEFNER, ALEX VS TENZOR, OC VS SHIVER FLAY.
VISUALES: MASA VS TOHYTO, KCHO VS C1RQA, HMTO.

   VOTA SIMPL3   we ♥ mujeres

Custom Font — Custom made for this project

Magazine Cover 2003 Switzerland   CL: soDA Magazine   AD, D: Marc Kappeler   I: Benjamin Güdel   DF, SB: moiré

Custom Font — Custom made for this project

Magazine Cover 2003 Switzerland   CL: soDA Magazine   AD: Marc Kappeler   D: Norm (green) / Happypets (silvergreen), Martin Woodtli (black), Marc Kappeler (red)   P: Katie Blitzer   DF, SB: moiré

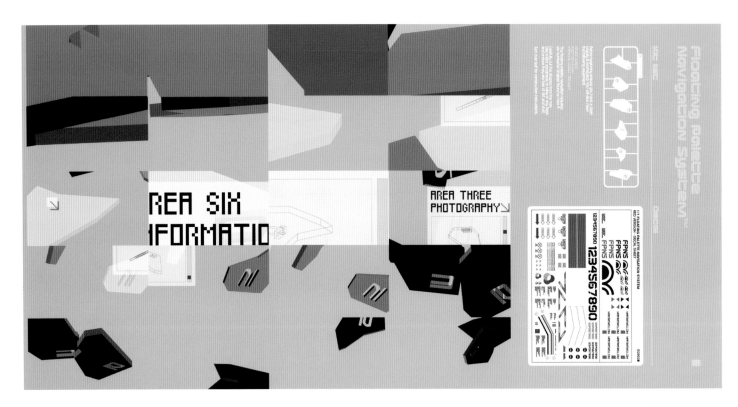

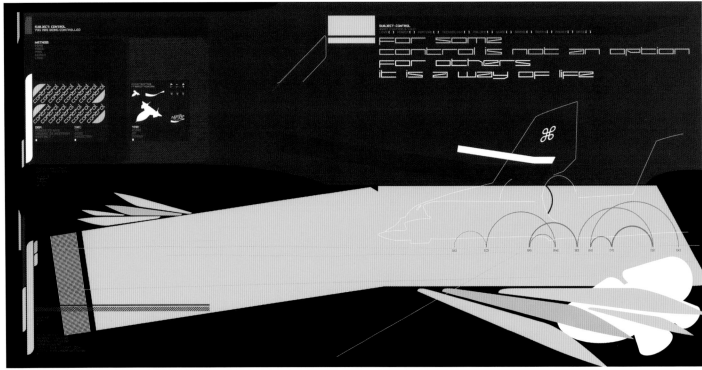

ABCDEFGHIJKLMNOPQRSTUVWXYZ abcdefghijklmnopqrstuvwxyz

p134, 136

Commercial Font   ⊞ Mechwar / Synthesis / Turbo   ⬇ http://www.t26.com (T26) / http://www.unionfonts.com (UnionFonts) / http://www.myfonts.com (Myfonts)

Original Works 2003 UK   AD, D, I, SB: Martin Fewell

ABCDEFGHIJKLMNOPQRSTUVWXYZ abcdefghijklmnopqrstuvwxyz

p134

Commercial Font   ⊞ Airframe / Airbrake / Nova   ⬇ http://www.t26.com (T26) / http://www.unionfonts.com (UnionFonts) / http://www.myfonts.com (Myfonts)

Original Works 2003 UK   AD, D, I, SB: Martin Fewell

LIQUIDROOM PRESENTS 2002-2003 NEW YEAR'S PARTY

dj **TAKKYU ISHINO**
(LOOPA RECORDINGS)
KAITO
(a.k.a. HIROSHI WATANABE)

live **CO-FUSION**
(REEL MUSIQ / SUBLIME)

vj **NAOHIRO UKAWA**
(MOM/N/DAD PRODUCTIONS)

2003-12-31 NEW YEAR'S EVE at LIQUIDROOM door open : 20:00 adv : ¥5000 (after 27:00am·¥3500/after 30:00am·¥3000)
TICKETS : selling start 12-8(SUN) at PIA, LAWSON, CISCO TECHNO, TECHNIQUE, LIQUIDROOM & more... info : http://www.liquidroom.net/

ABCDEFGHIJKLMNOPQRSTUVWXYZ abcdefghijklmnopqrstuvwxyz

Commercial Font   Mao Font / Hand Lettering   http://www.hamada-takeshi.com/portfolio/store/mao/mao.html
Poster 2002 Japan CL: Liquidroom Shinjuku AD, D, SB: Takeshi Hamada

Permutations
Kunstenaars: Jef Guess en Anne Marie Cornu
Vrijdag 4 april 13.00-17.00 uur
Zaterdag 5 april 16.00-20.00 uur (opening)
Zondag 6 april van 13.00-16.00 uur
De Franse kunstenaars Anne Marie Cornu en
Jeff Guess presenteren in Artis hun werk Permutations. **Permutations** is een collectie korte
filmfragmenten van filmers en kunstenaars. Deze
fragmenten zijn in een database gerangschikt in
een aantal categorieën. Deze vormen de bron
voor onuitputtelijke simultane projectievarianten.
In tegenstelling tot de speelfilm waarin het
verloop lineair en onveranderlijk is, biedt **Permutations** de mogelijkheid om de fragmenten
iedere keer anders te gebruiken en te interpre-
teren. Ieder fragment opent mogelijkheden voor
steeds andere projectiecombinaties. Dit resul-
teert in beeldassociaties die op groot formaat
op diverse schermen de ruimte van Artis zullen
transformeren.

Drukwerk: bi»lo, Den Bosch

ABCDEFGHJJKLMNOPQRSZUVWXYZ abcdeßghjjklmnopqrstuvwxyz

Free Font   ◼ File Sharing font / Kabel   ⬇ http://www.howtoplays.nl

Invitation Flyer 2003 Netherlands CL: Artis, Den Bosch AD, D, SB: Richard Niessen

SPOREN

DANS & MUSIEK

MUSICI
JOSEPH SCHLESINGER – COUNTERTENOR
FREEK BORSTLAP – VIOLA DA GAMBA
IVANKA NEELEMAN – VIOLA DA GAMBA
REINIER VAN HOUDT – PIANO

KOSTUUMS – AZIZ

DANS: ALBA BARRAL FERNANDEZ TY BOOMERSHINE _ JEFTA VAN DINTHER | HIWAKO ISHINO | TIM PERSENT ___ | LIA POOLE HEATHER WARE

LEINE ROEBANA

INFO: 020-4893820
DANS@LEINEROEBANA.COM
WWW.LEINEROEBANA.COM

FOTO:DEEN VAN MEER ONTWERP:KOEWEIDENPOSTMA (ALVIN CHAN)

Free Font   Webdings
Poster 2004 Holland CL: Leine Roebana AD: Alvin Chan P: Deen van Meer DF, SB: Koeweiden Postma

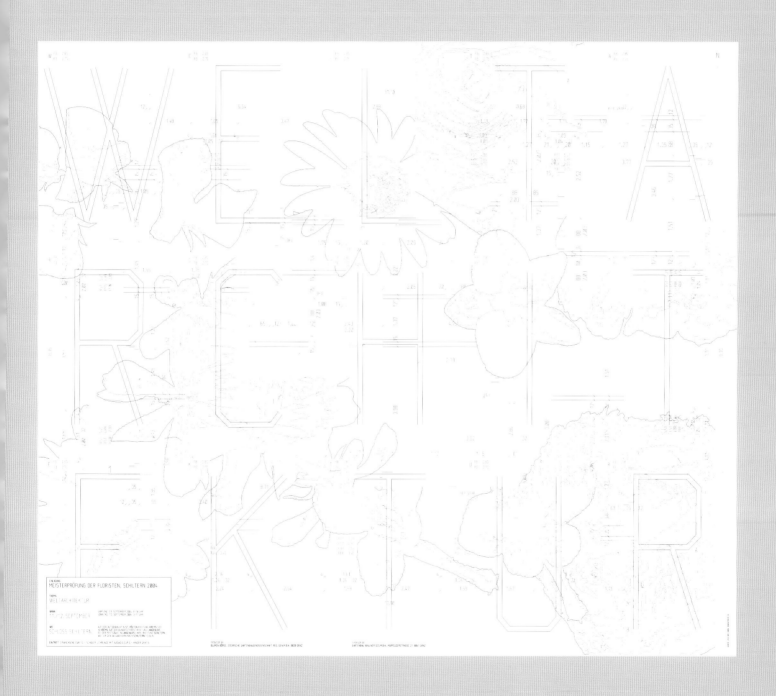

ABCDEFGHIJKLMNOPQRSTUVWXYZ abcdefghijklmnopqrstuvwxyz

Free Font   ▣ Schaltkreis   ⬇ http://www.mixer.ch

Poster, Invitation 2004 Switzerland   CL: Meisterklasse Schiltern   AD: Erich Brechbuhl   D: Erich Brechbuhl   DF, SB: Mixer

ABCDEFGHIJKLMNOPQRSTUVWXYZ abcdefghijklmnopqrstuvwxyz

Commercial Font   CA AiresPro-Regular / CA AiresPro-Italic   http://www.cape-arcona.com

CD 2004 Germany   CL: Quartermania Records   AD, D: Stefan Claudius   P: Nannette Römer   DF, SB: Claudius Design

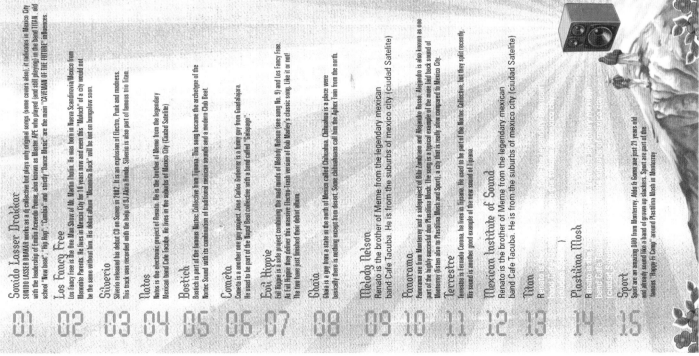

ABCDEFGHIJKLMNOPQRSTUUWXYZ abcdefghijklmnopqrstuvwxyz

Commercial Font   LED Gothic   http://www.t26.com

CD 2003 México   CL: Bungalow Records   AD, P, DF, SB: Hula+Hula   D: Quique Ollervides / Cha! & Oscar Reyes

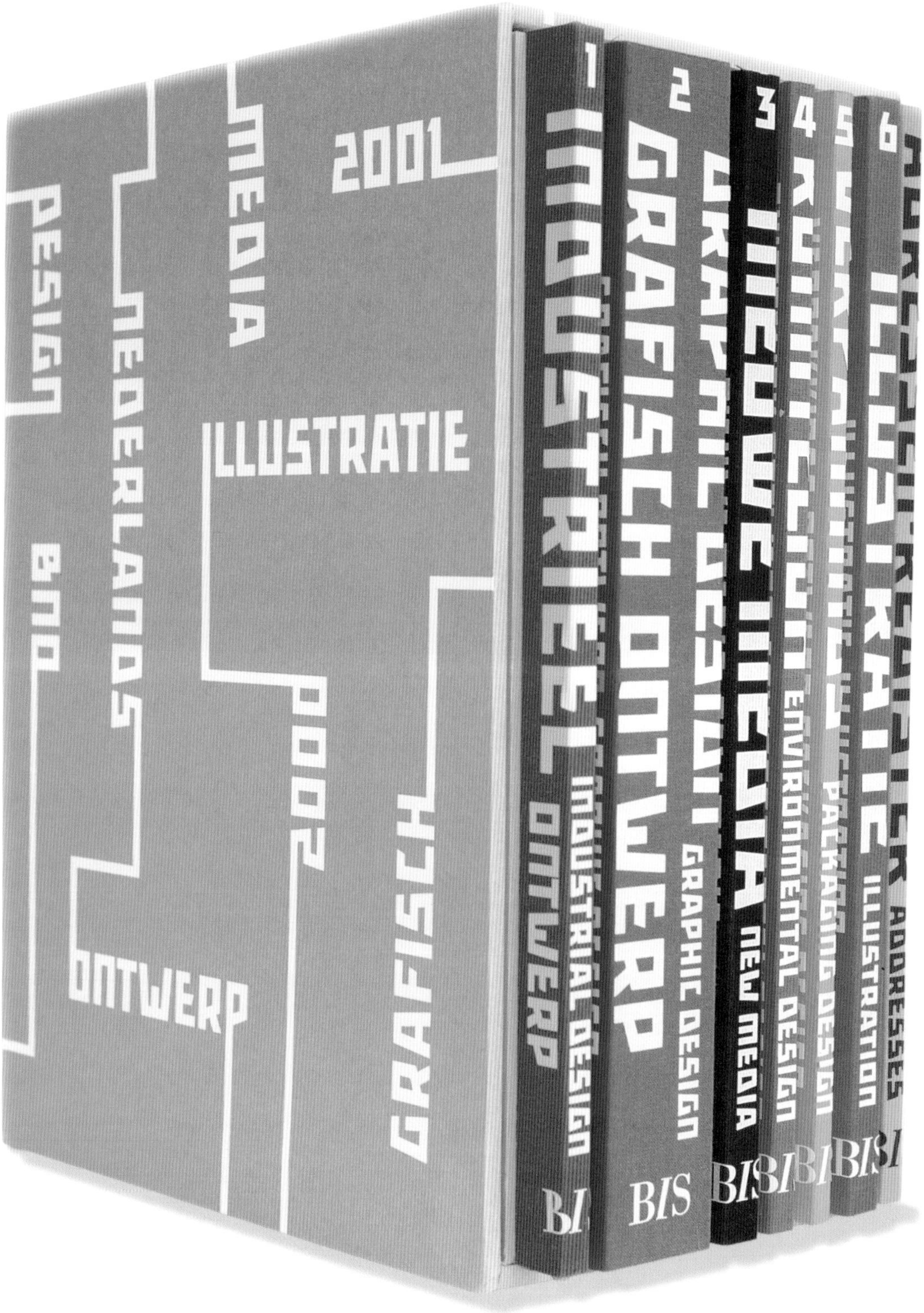

Custom Font

F BNO Alphabet / Environmental Bitmap Alphabet / Illustrative Alphabet etc.

Book 2000 Netherlands CL: BNO and Bis Publishers D, DF, SB: Atelier René Knip

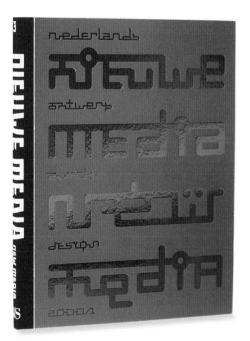

ABCDEFGHIJ
KLMNOPQRST
UVWXYZ·!?Œ
0123456789

Custom Font   ▪ Hema Ceramic Tile Alphabet

Interior Graphics 1997 Netherlands   CL: Merkx+Girod Architects   D, DF, SB: Atelier René Knip

ABCDEFGHI
JKLMNOPQR
STUVWXYJZ

Custom Font	F Environmental Bitmap Alphabet

Sign, Interior Graphics 2003 Netherlands   CL: Merkx+Girod Architects   D, DF, SB: Atelier René Knip

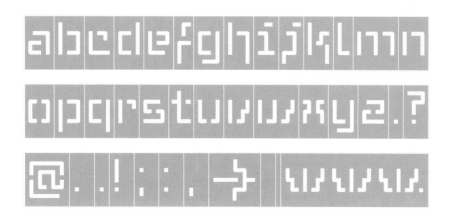

Custom Font • Gebr. Knip Type Lamp Alphabet

Installation 2004 Netherlands CL: Gebr.Knip D, DF, SB: Atelier René Knip

FONT
SAMPLES

ABCDEFGHIJKLMNOPQRST

UVWXYZ

abcdefghijklmnopqrstuvwxyz

0123456789@!?&.,

Commercial Font | 062aPlotter-Achtundzwanzig >>> http://www.forhomeorofficeuse.com | SB: VIER5 | p010

ABCDEFGHIJKLMNOPQRST

UVWXYZ

abcdefghijklmnopqrstuvwxyz

0123456789@!?&.,

Commercial Font | 062aPlotter-Bandzug >>> http://www.forhomeorofficeuse.com | SB: VIER5 | p012, 080

ABCDEFGHIJKLMNOPQRST

UVWXYZ

abcdefghijklmnopqrstuvwxyz

0123456789@!?&.,

Commercial Font | Capibara Normal >>> http://www.garagefonts.com/ | SB: GarageFonts | p101

ABCDEFGHIJKLMN
OPQRSTUVWXYZ
abcdefghijklmn
opqrstuvwxyz
0123456789@!?&.,

ABCDEFGHIJK
LMNOPQRSTUU
WXYZ

ABCDEFGHIJKLMNO
PQRSTUVWXYZ

Commercial Font | FT-Bold >>> http://www.forhomeorofficeuse.com | SB: VIER5 | p037

ABCDEFGHIJKLMNOPQRST
UVWXYZ
abcdefghijklmnopqrstuvwxyz
0123456789o!?£..

Commercial Font | 8Try-micro >>> http://www.forhomeorofficeuse.com | SB: VIER5

ABCDEFGHIJKLMNOPQRST
UVWXYZ
ABCDEFGHIJKLMNOPQRSTUVWXYZ
0123456789@??.

Commercial Font | Satellite >>> http://www.final.nu | SB: New Emit | p085

ABCDEFGHIJKLMNO
PQRSTUVWXYZ
abcdefghijklmnopqrstuvwxyz
0123456789@!?&

ABCDEFGHIJKLMNOPQRST
UVWXYZ
abcdefghijklmnopqrstuvwxyz
0123456789@!?$.,

ABCDEFGHIJKLMNOP
QRSTUVWXYZ
abcdefghijklmnop
qrstuvwxyz
0123456789@!?&.,

ABCDEFGHIJKLMNOPQRST
UVWXYZ
abcdefghijklmnopqrstuvwxyz
0123456789@!?&.,

ABCDEFGHIJKLMNOPQRST
UVWXYZ
abcdefghijklmnopqrstuvwxyz
0123456789@!?&.,

ABCDEFGHIJKLMNOPQRST
UVWXYZ
abcdefghijklmnopqrstuvwxyz
0123456789@!?&.,

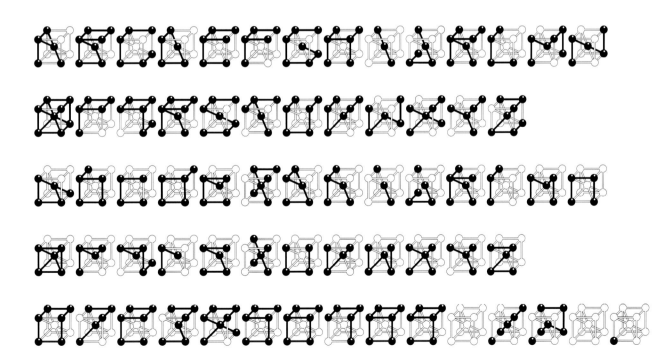

ABCDEFGHIJKLMNOPQRST
UVWXYZ
abcdefghijklmnopqrstuvwxyz
0123456789@!?&.,

ABCDEFGHIJKLMNOPQRST
UVWXYZ
abcdefghijklmnopqrstuvwxyz
0123456789@!?&.,

ABCDEFGHIJKLMNOPQRST
UVWXYZ
abcdefghijklmnopqrstuvwxyz
0123456789@!?&.,

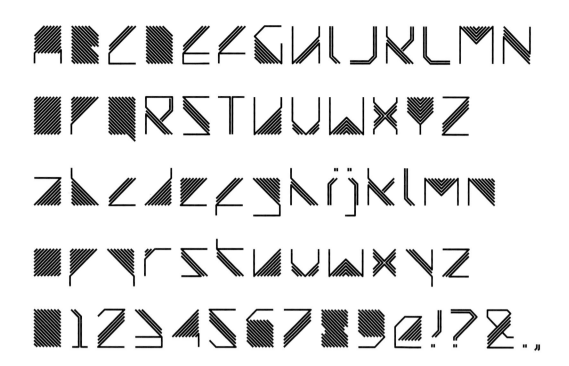

ABCDEFGHIJKLMNOPQRST
UVWXYZ
abcdefghijklmnopqrstuvwxyz
0123456789@!?&.,

Commercial Font | Assembler >>> http://www.t26.com | SB: Martin Fewell

ABCDEFGHIJKLMNOPQRSTUVWXYZ
abcdefghijklmnopqrstuvwxyz
0123456789@!?&.,

Commercial Font | BD Rainbow >>> http://www.typedifferent.com | SB: buro destruct

ABCDEFGHIJKLMNOPQRST
UVWXYZ
abcdefghijklmnopqrstuvwxyz
0123456789 .,

Commercial Font | Kryptonite >>> http://www.characters.nl | SB: René Verkaart

ABCDEFGHIJKLMN
OPQRSTUVWXYZ
ABCDEFGHIJKLMN
OPQRSTUVWXYZ
0123456789@!?&.,

ABCDEFGHIJKLMN
OPQRSTUVWXYZ
abcdefghijklmn
opqrstuvwxyz
0123456789@!?+.,

ABCDEFGHIJKLMNOPQRST
UVWXYZ
abcdefghijklmnopqrstuvwxyz
0123456789@!?&.,

Commercial Font | Nordic A Narrow Regular >>> http://www.fountain.nu | SB: René Verkaart

ABCDEFGHIJKLMNÑOPQRST
UVWXYZ
ABCDEFGHIJKLMNÑOPQRSTUVWXYZ
0123456789@!?&.,

Commercial Font | Unplugged! >>> http://www.unionfonts.com | SB: Dr. Alderete | p107

ABCDEFGHIJKLMNÑOPQRST
UVWXYZ
0123456789 !?&.

Commercial Font | Platillo Volador >>> http://www.unionfonts.com | SB: Dr. Alderete | p107

ABCDEFGHIJKLMN
OPQRSTUVWXYZ
abcdefghijklmn
opqrstuvwxyz
0123456789@!?&..

ABCDEFGHIJKLMN
OPQRSTUVWXYZ
ABCDEFGHIJKLMN
OPQRSTUVWXYZ
0123456789@!?&▦●

ABCDEFGHIJKLMNOPQRST
UVWXYZ
abcdefghijklmnopqrstuvwxyz
0123456789@!?&.,

Commercial Font | CA Geheimagent - Normal >>> http://www.cape-arcona.com | SB: Claudius Design | p084

ABCDEFGHIJKLMNOPQRST
UVWXYZ
abcdefghijklmnopqrstuvwxyz
0123456789@!?&.,

Commercial Font | CA BND >>> http://www.cape-arcona.com | SB: Cape Arcona Type Foundry | p086

ABCDEFGHIJKLMNOPQRST
UVWXYZ
abcdefghijklmnopqrstuvwxyz
0123456789@!?&.,

Commercial Font | CA AiresPro - Regular >>> http://www.cape-arcona.com | SB: Claudius Design | p120

ABCDEFGHIJKLMNOPQRST
UVWXYZ
abcdefghijklmnopqrstuvwxyz
0123456789@!?&.,

ABCDEFGHIJKLMNOPQRST
UVWXYZ
abcdefghijklmnopqrstuvwxyz
0123456789@!?&.,

ABCDEFGHIJKLMNOPQRST
UVWXYZ
abcdefghijklmnopqrstuvwxyz
0123456789@!?&.,

ABCDEFGHIJKLMNOPQRST
UVWXYZ
ABCDEFGHIJKLMNOPQRSTUVWXYZ
0123456789 @!*&.,

abcdefghijklmnopqrst
uvwxyz
abcdefghijklmnopqrstuvwxyz
0123456789 @!?&.,

ABCDEFGHIJKLMNOPQRST
UVWXYZ
abcdefghijklmnopqrstuvwxyz
0123456789@!?&.,

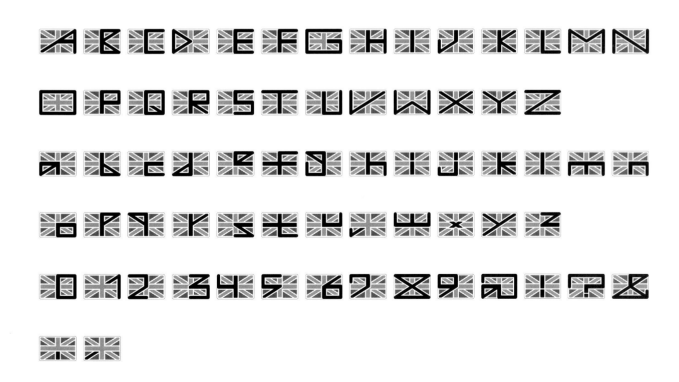

Custom Font | ARBM | SB: Richard Niessen | p022-025

Custom Font | TM | SB: Richard Niessen | p046-048

Custom Font | Moment >>> http://www.ohminato.com/ | SB: Kazuaki Ohminato

ABCDEFGHIJKLMN
OPQRSTUVWXYZ
abcdefghijklmn
opqrstuvwxyz
0123456789

abcdefghijk
lmnopqrstu
vwxyz

Custom Font | aleph | SB: Studio Apeloig | p087

abcdefghijklm
nopqrstu
vwxyz

Custom Font | octobre | SB: Studio Apeloig

ABCDEFG HIJKLMNOPQRST
UVWXYZ

ABCDEFG HIJKLMNOPQRSTUVWXYZ
0123456789 @!?&.,

Custom Font | tublar | SB: MASA | p106

ABCDEFGHIJKLMNOPQRST
UVWXYZ
abcdefghijklmnopqrstuvwxyz
0123456789!?&.,

ABCDEFGHIJKLMNOPQRST
UVWXYZ
0123456789@!?&.,

ABCDEFGHIJKLMNOPQRST
UVWXYZ
abcdefghijklmnopqrstuvwxyz
0123456789@!?&.,

ABCDEFGHIJKLMNOPQRST
UVWXYZ

ABCDEFGHIJKLMNOPQRST
0123456789 @ !?&.,

ABCDEFGHIJKLMNOPQRST
UVWXYZ

ABCDEFGHIJKLMNOPQRSTUVWXYZ
0123456789 @ !?&.,

ABCDEFGHIJKLMNOPQRST
UVWXYZ

ABCDEFGHIJKLMNOPQRSTUVWXYZ
0123456789&!?&.,

ABCDEFGHIJKLMNOPQRSTUVWYZ
UVWYZ

ABCDEFGHIJKLMNOPQRSTUVWYZ
0123456789 @ !?&.,

Custom Font   CHACHOPO   SB: MASA

ABCDEFGHIJKLMNOPQRST UVWXYZ

abcdefghijklmnopqrstuvwxyz
0123456789@!?&.,

Custom Font   Roofters >>> http://www.fellowdesigners.com   SB: Fellow Designers

ABCDEFGHIJKLMNOPQRST UVWXYZ

abcdefghijklmnopqrstuvwxyz
0123456789@!?&.,

Custom Font   Common Ground >>> http://www.ohminato.com/   SB: Kazuaki Ohminato

ABCDEFGHIJKLMNOP
QRSTUVWXYZ
abcdefghijklmnopqrst
uvwxyz
0123456789@!?&.,

ABCDEFGHIJKLMNOPQRST
UVWXYZ
abcdefghijklmnopqrstuvwxyz
0123456789@!?&.,

ABCDEFGHIJKLMNOPQRSTUVWXYZ
abcdefghijklmnopqrstuvwxyz
0123456789@!?&.,

ABCDEFGHIJKLMNOPQRST
UVWXYZ
abcdefghijklmnopqrstuvwxyz
0123456789 @ !?&.,

ABCDEFGHIJKLMNOPQRST
UVWXYZ
ABCDEFGHIJKLMNOPQRSTUVWXYZ
0123456789@!?&.,

abcdefghijklmnopqrst
uvwxyz
abcdefghijklmnopqrstuvwxyz
0123456789 @ !?&.,

ABCDEFGHIJKLMNOPQRSTUVWXYZ
abcdefghijklmnopqrstuvwxyz
0123456789!?.,

Free Font | Schaltkreis >>> http://www.mixer.ch | SB: Mixer | p119

ABCDEFGHIJKLMNOPQRSTUVWXYZ
ABCDEFGHIJKLMNOPQRSTUVWXYZ
0123456789!?&.,

Free Font | BD BDRmono >>> http://www.typedifferent.com | SB: buro destruct | p109

ABCDEFGHIJKLMNOPQRST
UVWXYZ
ABCDEFGHIJKLMNOPQRSTUVWXYZ
0123456789 !?&.,

Free Font | Encrypted Wallpaper >>> http://www.characters.nl | SB: René Verkaart

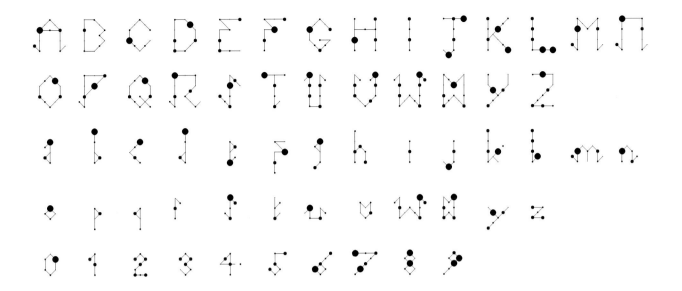

ABCDEFGHIJKLMNOPQRST
UVWXYZ
ABCDEFGHIJKLMNOPQRSTUVWXYZ

ABCDEFGHIJKLMN
OPQRSTUVWXYZ
0123456789@!?+.,

ABCDEFGHIJKLMN
OPQRSTUVWXYZ
abcdefghijklmnopq
rstuvwxyz
0123456789@!?&.,

ABCDEFGHIJKLMN
OPQRSTUVWXYZ
abcdefghijklmn
opqrstuvwxyz
0123456789 ! ? . ,

ABCDEFGHIJKLMN
OPQRSTUVWXYZ
ABCDEFGHIJKLMN
OPQRSTUVWXYZ
0123456789Ø!?£.,

abcdefghijklmnopqrst
uvwxyz&&
abcdefghijklmnopqrstuvwxyz&&
123456789 123456789

ABCDEFGHIJKLMNOPQRST
UVWXYZ
abcdefghijklmnopqrstuvwxyz
0123456789a!??..

abcdefghijklmn
opqrstuvwxyz
0123456789@!?&.,

SUBMITTORS'
INDEX

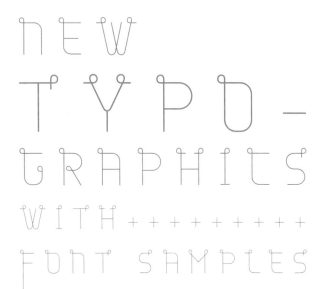

NEW TYPO-GRAPHICS WITH +++++++++ FONT SAMPLES

Designer : Hajime Kabutoya

Coordinator / Translator : Maya Kishida

Editor : Hitoshi Mitomi

Publisher : Shingo Miyoshi

First edition, first issue January 21, 2005

Published by PIE BOOKS

2-32-4, Minami-Otsuka, Toshima-ku, Tokyo 170-0005, Japan
Sales : Tel:+81-3-5395-4811 Fax:+81-3-5395-4812 e-mail: sales@piebooks.com
Editor : Tel:+81-3-5395-4820 Fax:+81-3-5395-4821 e-mail: editor@piebooks.com
http://www.piebooks.com

Printing and binding : TOSHO PRINTING CO., LTD.

デザイン：甲谷 一

コーディネイター / 翻訳：岸田麻矢

編集：三富 仁

発行人：三芳伸吾

2005年1月21日　初版第1刷発行

発行所：ピエ・ブックス

〒170-0005 東京都豊島区南大塚2-32-4
営業：Tel: 03-5395-4811 Fax: 03-5395-4812 e-mail: sales@piebooks.com
編集：Tel: 03-5395-4820 Fax: 03-5395-4821 e-mail: editor@piebooks.com
http://www.piebooks.com

印刷・製本：図書印刷株式会社

ニュー タイポグラフィックス 書体見本付

TRAVEL & LEISURE GRAPHICS 2

トラベル＆レジャー グラフィックス 2

Pages: 224 (Full Color)　¥15,000+Tax

ホテル、旅館、観光地、交通機関からアミューズメント施設までのグラフィックス約350点を一挙掲載！！パンフレットを中心にポスター、DM、カードなど…現地へ行かなければ入手困難な作品も含め紹介。資料としてそろえておきたい1冊です！

A richly varied selection of 350 samples of travel and leisure guide graphics. The collection conveniently presents tour information, sightseeing guides, posters, promotional pamphlets from airline, railroad companies, hotels, inns, facilities, and more. Pick up this one-volume reference, and have it all at your fingertrips without having to leave your seat, let alone leave town!

PICTOGRAM AND ICON GRAPHICS

ピクトグラム＆アイコン グラフィックス

Pages: 200 (160 in Color)　¥13,000+Tax

ミュージアムや空港の施設案内表示から雑誌やWEBサイトのアイコンまで、業種別に分類し、実用例とともに紹介しています。ピクトグラムの意味や使用用途などもあわせて紹介した、他に類をみないまさに永久保存版の1冊です。

The world's most outstanding pictograms and applications. From pictographs seen in museums, airports and other facility signage to icons used in magazines and on the web, the examples are shown isolated and in application with captions identifying their meanings and uses. Categorized by industry for easy reference, no other book of its kind is as comprehensive—it is indeed a permanent archives in one volume!

NEW COMPANY BROCHURE DESIGN 2

ニュー カンパニー ブローシャー デザイン 2

Pages: 272 (Full Color)　¥15,000+Tax

デザインの優れた案内カタログ約150点とWEB約50点を厳選。WEBサイトはカタログと連動した作品を中心に紹介しています。また各作品の企画・構成内容がわかるように制作コンセプト・コンテンツのキャッチコピーを具体的に掲載しています。

A selection of over 150 superbly designed brochures and 50 corresponding websites. All works are accompanied by descriptions of their design objectives and catch copy, to provide added insight into their planning and compositional structures.

ENVIRONMENT/WELFARE-RELATED GRAPHICS

環境・福祉 グラフィックス

Pages: 240 (Full Color)　¥15,000+Tax

環境保全への配慮が世界的な常識となりつつある今日、企業も積極的に環境・福祉など社会的テーマを中心にした広告キャンペーンを展開しています。国内外の優れた環境・福祉広告を紹介した本書は今後の広告を考えるために必携の1冊となるでしょう。

Environmental conservation is now a worldwide concern, and corporate advertising campaigns based on environmental and social themes are on the rise. This collection of noteworthy local and international environment/welfare-related publicity is an essential reference for anyone involved in the planning and development of future advertising.

PAPER IN DESIGN

ペーパー イン デザイン

Pages: 192 (Full Color) + Special reference material (paper samples)　¥16,000+Tax

DM、カタログをはじめ書籍の装丁、商品パッケージなど、紙素材を利用し個性的な効果を上げている数多くの作品をアイテムにこだわらず紹介。掲載作品で使われている紙見本も添付、紙のテクスチャーを実際に確かめることができる仕様です。

A special collection of graphic applications that exploit the role paper plays in design. This collection presents a wide range of applications—DM, catalogs, books, and product packaging, etc.—in which paper is used to achieve unique visual statements. Actual paper samples accompany each work to demonstrate their texture and tactile qualities.

BUSINESS PUBLICATION STYLE

PR誌企画&デザイン 年間ケーススタディ

Pages: 224 (Full Color)　¥15,000+Tax

PR誌の年間企画スケジュールとビジュアル展開を1年分まとめて紹介します。特集はどういう内容で構成しているのか？エッセイの内容と執筆人は？など、創刊・リニューアル時の企画段階から役立つ待望の1冊です。

Year-long case studies of 40 critically selected PR magazines.What should the content of the feature stories composed ? What should the subject of the essays be and who should write them? This eagerly awaited collection promises to assist in the planning stages for the inauguration or renewal of business periodicals.

SMALL PAMPHLET GRAPHICS

スモール パンフレット グラフィックス

Pages: 224 (Full Color)　¥14,000+Tax

街や店頭で見かける様々な企業、ショップのパンフレットを衣・食・住・遊の業種別に紹介します。気軽に持ち帰ることができる数多くの小型パンフレットの中からデザイン性に優れた作品約300点を厳選しました。

A collection introducing a wide variety of company and shop pamphlets found in stores and around town, grouped under the categories "food, clothes, shelter, and entertainment." 300 small-scale pamphlets selected for their outstanding design qualities from the great many pieces available to customers for the taking.

NEW CALENDAR GRAPHICS

ニュー カレンダー グラフィックス

Pages: 224 (Full Color)　¥13,000+Tax

国内外のクリエイターから集めた個性豊かなカレンダー約200点を、企業プロモーション用、市販用と目的別に収録した、世界の最新カレンダーを特集！！カレンダーの制作現場に、欠かすことの出来ない実用性の高い一冊です。

Over 200 of the newest and most original calendars from designers around the world! Categorized by objective, this collection includes calendars for the retail market as well as those designed as corporate publicity pieces.

NEW ENCYCLOPEDIA OF PAPER-FOLDING DESIGNS

折り方大全集 DM・カタログ編

Page: 240 (160 in Color) ¥7,800+Tax

デザインの表現方法の1つとして使われている『折り』。日頃何げなく目にしているDMやカード、企業のプロモーション用カタログなど身近なデザイン中に表現されている『折り』から、たたむ機能やせり出す、たわめる機能まで、約200点の作品を展開図で示し、『折り』を効果的に生かした実際の作品を掲載しています。

Morc than 200 examples of direct mail, cards, and other familiar printed materials featuring simple / multiple folds, folding up, and insertion shown as they are effected by folding along with flat diagrams of their prefolded forms.

SMALL JAPANESE STYLE GRAPHICS

スモールジャパン スタイル グラフィックス

Page: 224 (Full Color) ¥15,000+Tax

日本伝統の文様・イラスト・色彩等、和のテイストが随所にちりばめられたグラフィック作品を1冊にまとめました。古き良き日本の美意識を取り入れ、現代のクリエイターが仕上げた作品は新しい和の感覚を呼びさまします。

Traditional Japanese motifs, illustrations, colors—collection of graphicworks studded with the essence of "wa" (Japanese-ness) on every page. See how contemporary Japanese designers incorporate time-honored Japanese aesthetics in finished works that redefine the sensibility known as "Japanese style."

LAYOUT STYLE GRAPHICS

レイアウト スタイル グラフィックス

Pages: 224 (Full Color) ¥14,000+Tax

カタログや雑誌などのレイアウトをする上で必要不可欠な、目次や扉ページ・ノンブル・柱などの細かい要素。本書はそれらをパーツごとにコンテンツわけして、優れた作品例を紹介します。美しいレイアウトを作成するための参考資料として、グラフィックデザイナー必携の一冊となるはずです。

Table of contents and title pages, pagination,titles, &c. —these are the essential elements of catalog and magazine layout. This collection presents outstanding examples of editorial design broken down and categorized by their key components. A volume that will prove indispensable to graphic designers as a reference for creating beautiful layouts.

IDEAS UNBOUND

自由なアイデア & 表現 グラフィックス

Pages: 224 (Full Color) ¥14,000+Tax

本書はコンセプトに基づきアイデアを生かしグラフィック表現されたもの、紙やその他の素材の特徴をうまく生かし表現したもの、最新または超アナログ印刷技術を駆使した作品などを特集したデザイナーのアイデアの宝庫ともいえる必須の一冊です。

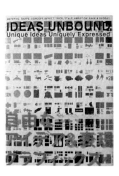

This book focuses on conceptual graphic works that exploit the characteristics of paper and other materials to express those ideas, a collection of latest, "state-of-the-art" analog printing techniques and a treasure trove of designers' ideas-a must for anyone who appreciates creative genius.

EVERYDAY DIAGRAM GRAPHICS

エブリデイ ダイアグラム グラフィックス

Page: 224 (Full Color) ¥14,000+Tax

本書はわかりやすいということにポイントを置き、私たちの身の回りや街で見かける身近なダイアグラムを特集しました。マップ・フロアガイド・チャート・グラフ・仕様書など、わかりやすいだけでなく、見ていて楽しいものを紹介しています。

This collection features diagrams of the sort we constantly meet in our daily lives, selected with their ready 'digestibility' in mind. The maps, charts, graphs, floor guides and specifications introduced here are not just easy to understand, they're fun to look at, too.

SCHOOL & FACILITY PROSPECTUS GRAPHICS

学校・施設案内 グラフィックス

Pages: 224 (Full Color) ¥15,000+Tax

「学校」「施設」という2つの大きなコンテンツを軸に、デザイン、企画、コンセプトに優れたカタログ、リーフレットなどの案内ツールを収録。表紙、中ページのレイアウト、構成からキャッチコピーまで見やすく紹介しています。

A collection presenting examples of well-designed and conceptually outstanding guides (catalogs, pamphlets, leaflets, etc) focusing on two broad categories: schools and service facilities. Documentation includes cover and inside pages, highlighting layout, composition, and catch copy.

A4 IN-STORE LEAFLET GRAPHICS

店頭 A4リーフレット グラフィックス

Pages: 224 (Full Color) ¥15,000+Tax

様々な業種の店頭に置かれた販促用のA4・B5サイズのペラ物や2つ折り、3つ折りのチラシ・リーフレットに限定し約650点を収録。デザイナーを悩ます、文字や写真などの構成要素の多い実務的なリーフレットの効果的な見せ方がわかる1冊です。

A collection featuring 650 flat, single- and double-fold A4 and B5 sized leaflets found in retail environments, representing a wide range of businesses. This single volume presents effective examples of the practical business tool that because of its many compositional elements always poses a challenge to designers.

BRAND STRATEGY AND DESIGN

ブランド戦略とデザイン

Page: 224 (208 in Color) ¥15,000+Tax

「ブランド戦略」にデザイナーが参加することは規模の大小を問わず求められています。今後デザイナーは総合的に戦略を考える力が必要です。本書はデザイナーが積極的にブランド戦略に関わることで認知度アップに貢献した実例を紹介します。

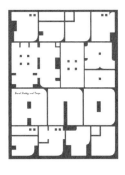

In projects big and small, designers are being called upon to participate in "brand strategy". In coming years, designers will require the ability to consider brand strategy comprehensively. This book presents case studies in which the designer's active role in brand strategy contributed to a higher degree of brand recognition.

ADVERTISING PHOTOGRAPHY IN JAPAN 2004

年鑑 日本の広告写真2004

Pages: 229 (Full Color)　¥14,500+Tax

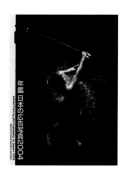

気鋭の広告写真をそろえた（社）日本広告写真家協会（APA）の監修による本年鑑は、日本の広告界における最新のトレンドと、その証言者たる作品を一堂に見られる貴重な資料として、国内外の広告に携わる方にとって欠かせない存在です。

A spirited collection of works compiled under the editorial supervision of the Japan Advertising Photographers' Association (APA) representing the freshest talent in the Japanese advertising world. An indispensable reference for anyone concerned with advertising in or outside Japan.

ADVERTISING GRAPHICS WITH IMPACT

インパクトのある広告グラフィックス

Page: 224 (Full Color)　¥14,000+Tax

ポスターを中心に雑誌広告などから、コミカルで笑いを誘う作品、衝撃的で目を引く作品、意表をつく奇抜な作品、豪快で驚異的な作品などを紹介。五感に訴え、心に強く残り、高い広告効果をあげているインパクトのある作品の特集です。

A collection of select world advertising with IMPACT! Laughter-provoking comical works, attention-getting shocking works, unconventional works that take viewers by surprise. A collection of primarily poster and magazine ad graphics that appeal to the five senses, demonstrating a wide range of ways to have IMPACT.

NEW SEASONAL CAMPAIGN GRAPHICS

季節別 キャンペーンツール グラフィックス

Page: 224 (Full Color)　¥15,000+Tax

企業やショップが展開している様々なキャンペーンの中からクリスマス、お正月、バレンタイン、母の日、父の日、サマー・ウィンターセールなど、特に季節を感じさせるものに対象をしぼり、そこで使用された優れたデザインの販促ツールやノベルティグッズを紹介します。

Christmas, New Year's, Valentine's Day, Mother's and Father's Day, summer and winter sales, &c, this collection presents outstandingly designed corporate and retail campaign materials and novelties with a season-specific focus.

PACKAGE & WRAPPING GRAPHICS

パッケージ & ラッピングツール グラフィックス

Page: 224 (Full Color)　¥14,000+Tax

様々な商品パッケージには、販売対象やブランドイメージに沿ったデザイン戦略がなされており、商品イメージを決定する重要な役割を担っています。本書は世界中からデザイン性の高いパッケージとラッピングツールを多数ピックアップし、食・美容・住にコンテンツわけして紹介しています。

Package is based on carefully developed design strategies to appeal to target customers and to build brand and protect image. This collection presents a wide variety of packages and wrapping materials from around the world reflecting the state of the art. It is grouped loosely under the categories food, beauty and living.

ENVIRONMENTAL COMMUNICATION GRAPHICS

環境コミュニケーションツール グラフィックス

Page: 224 (Full Color)　¥14,000+Tax

環境リポートや、環境をテーマとしたリーフレット、チラシ、ポスターなど、環境コミュニケーション・ツールを一堂に会し、業種別に紹介します。本書は、会社案内や各種パンフレット制作などあらゆるクリエイティブのアイデアソースとしても、利用価値の高い1冊です。

This book provides an overview of environmental communications tools, including leaflets, handbills and posters that focus on the topic of the environment, classifying them by type of business. This book is indeed a valuable source of creative ideas that graphic artists can use in creating company brochures and many other brochures.

DIRECT MAIL COMMUNICATIONS

ダイレクトメール コミュニケーション

Pages: 224 (Full Color)　¥14,000+Tax

本書は、顧客とのダイレクトなコミュニケーション・ツールとして活用する、様々な招待状、案内状をまとめたデザイン書です。伝えたい情報が、美しく、分かりやすくデザインされているものや、顧客の遊び心をくすぐるための、仕掛けのあるものなど、様々なタイプのダイレクトメールを多数収録します。

A design book focusing on invitations and announcements designed to function as communications tools that speak directly to their target customer. This collection presents a wide variety of direct mail pieces that deliver their messages beautifully, loud and clear, with tricks and devices, by tickling the playful spirit, and many other unique and interesting ways.

PUBLIC RELATIONS GRAPHICS

パブリック リレーションズ グラフィックス

Page: 224 (Full Color)　¥15,000+Tax

企業、団体、店舗で発行されている多様な広報誌・PR誌・フリーペーパーを特集しています。人目を引く表紙、見やすいレイアウト、読まれる特集とは？ 表紙、中ページを見やすく紹介した本書は、デザイン・編集・企画にきっと役立つ1冊となるでしょう。

A special collection focusing on the various public relations magazines, bulletins and free newspapers published by companies, organizations and retailers. What makes eyecatching covers, visually accessible layouts, and features people read? The answers are obvious in the covers and inside pages presented in this single volume —certain to serve as a valuable reference to anyone involved in the design, editing, and planning.

DESIGN IDEAS WITH LIMITED COLOR

限られた色のデザインアイデア

Page: 208 (192 in Color)　¥13,000+Tax

限られた刷り色で効果的にデザインされた作品を、使用された刷り色の色見本・パントーン（DIC含む）ナンバーと併せて紹介。色の掛け合わせと濃度変化がわかるカラーチャートを併録。無限大のアイデアを探し出すときに必要となる1冊。

A collection of the latest graphic works effectively reproduced using limited ink colors. Presented with color swatches and the Pantone/DIC numbers of the ink colors used, gradation and duotone works also feature simple color charts indicating screen and density changes. A reference of limitless ideas for anyone specifying color.

WORLD CORPORATE PROFILE GRAPHICS

ニュー 世界の会社案内 グラフィックス

Page: 256 (Full Color) ¥14,000+Tax

世界から集めた最新の会社案内・学校・施設案内と
アニュアルレポートを業種別に紹介。作品を大きく
見せながらも形態、デザイン制作コンセプト、コン
テンツ内容を簡潔に掲載しています。世界のデザイ
ナーの動向を掴む上でも貴重な1冊です。

The latest exemplary company, school and institution
guides and annual reports collected from diversified
industries worldwide and grouped by line of business.
Shown large scale, the pieces are accompanied by
brief descriptions of their content and the concepts
behind their design. Valuable for gleaning the latest
trends in corporate communications.

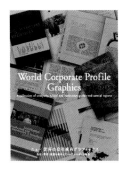

WORLD CATALOG EXPO

ワールド カタログ エキスポ

Page: 192 (Full Color) ¥5,800+Tax

一目でわかるように、衣食住のコンテンツは色分け
されています。高級感あるスマートな作品、楽しく
カラフルな作品、斬新なアイデアの作品など、ペー
ジをめくるごとに様々な作品の個性が広がる、国際
色豊かな1冊です。

A survey of outstanding catalogs from around the
world: simple and refined, colorful and playful, full of
novel ideas. Color-coded for easy identification
under the categories: Fashion, Food, and Living.
Highly original works, international in flavor, spill out
with each turn of the page.

GRAND OPENING GRAPHICS

オープン ツール グラフィックス

Pages: 216 (Full Color) ¥14,000+Tax

ショップや施設をオープンする際に制作するグラフ
ィックツールは、新しい「空間」のイメージを消費
者へ伝える大切な役割を果たします。本書ではオー
プン時に制作された案内状やショップツール、店舗
写真などを業種ごとに多数収録。

The graphic applications created for the openings of
new stores and facilities play a critical role in
conveying store image to customers. Categorized by
line of business, this book presents the wide range
of graphics — from invitations to in-store collateral –
that form the first impressions in building strategic
store identity.

FOOD SHOP GRAPHICS

フード ショップ グラフィックス

Page: 224 (Full Color) ¥14,000+Tax

レストラン・カフェ・菓子店など、国内外のオリジ
ナリティ溢れる飲食店のショップアイデンティティ
特集です。メニューやリーフレットなどのグラフィ
ックと、内装・外装の店舗写真、コンセプト文を交
え、約120店を紹介。

Restaurants, cafes, sweet shops... 120 of the world's
most original food-related store identities. Together
with graphic applications ranging from menus to
matches, each presentation features exterior and
interior photos of the shops and brief descriptions of
the concepts behind them.

OUTSTANDING SMALL PAMPHLET GRAPHICS

街で目立つ小型パンフレット

Pages: 240 (Full Color) ¥14,000+Tax

街やショップの店頭で手に入る無料の小型パンフ。
50ヶ所以上の街で集めた約1,000点から、販売促進
ツールとして効果的に機能している作品を厳選。
衣・食・住・遊の業種別に分類し機能的で美しい小
型パンフレットを約250点紹介します。

250 small-scale pamphlets selected for their beauty
and function as effective sales promotional tools from
roughly 1000 pieces available to customers at more
than 50 locations. Grouped for valuable reference by
type of business type under the categories: Food,
Clothing, Shelter, and Entertainment.

365 DAYS OF NEWSPAPER INSERTS Spring / Summer Edition

365日の折込チラシ大百科 春夏編

Page: 240 (Full Color) ¥13,000+Tax

全国の主要6都市から厳選された春夏の新聞折込チラ
シを一挙に掲載。優れたデザインや配色、目を引く
キャッチコピーの作品が満載。お正月、成人の日、
バレンタイン、お雛様、子供の日、母の日、父の日
などの作品を含む季節感溢れる1冊です。

Volume 3 of our popular series! Eye-catching
newspaper inserts – outstanding in design, color and
copywriting – selected from 6 major Japanese cities
between January and June. Brimming with the spirit
and events of spring: New Year's, Valentine's Day,
Girls'/Boys' Days, Mother's/Father's Days, and more.

カタログ・新刊のご案内について

総合カタログ、新刊案内をご希望の方は、はさみ込みのアンケートはがきを
ご返送いただくか、90円切手同封の上、ピエ・ブックス宛お申し込みください。

CATALOGUES ET INFORMATIONS SUR LES NOUVELLES PUBLICATIONS

Si vous désirez recevoir un exemplaire qratuit de notre catalogue généralou des
détails sur nos nouvelles publication. veuillez compléter la carte réponse incluse et
nous la retourner par courrierou par fax.

ピエ・ブックス

〒170-0005 東京都豊島区南大塚2-32-4
TEL: 03-5395-4811 FAX: 03-5395-4812
www.piebooks.com

CATALOGS and INFORMATION ON NEW PUBLICATIONS

If you would like to receive a free copy of our general catalog
or details of our new publications, please fill out the enclosed postcard
and return it to us by mail or fax.

CATALOGE und INFORMATIONEN ÜBER NEUE TITLE

Wenn Sie unseren Gesamtkatalog oder Detailinformationen über
unsere neuen Titel wünschen.fullen Sie bitte die beigefügte Postkarte aus
und schicken Sie sie uns per Post oder Fax.

PIE BOOKS

2-32-4 Minami-Otsuka Toshima-ku Tokyo 170-0005 JAPAN
TEL : +81-3-5395-4811 FAX : +81-3-5395-4812
www.piebooks.com